The Oldways 4-Week Vegetarian & Vegan Diet Menu Plan

Power Your Day With Wholesome Plant Foods!

Created by Oldways and Sharon Palmer, RD

D1510812

Special thanks to our sponsors and partners, whose support and generosity have made this book possible: Bob's Red Mill; Daisy Brand; Del Monte; Hass Avocado Board; Meatless Monday; The Peanut Institute; Produce for Better Health Foundation; Silk; Soyfoods Association of North America; Veggiecation; and Westbrae. Special appreciation to Kelli Swensen, Dietetic Intern, Newton Wellesley Hospital, for helping with the nutritional analysis.

For information on special discounts for bulk purchases
or opportunities to co-brand this book for your patients, clients,
or customers, please contact store@oldwayspt.org.

ISBN 978-0-9858939-2-7

Every effort has been made to ensure that the information in this book is complete and accurate. However, this book is not intended as a substitute for consulting with your physician. All matters regarding your health require medical supervision. The authors will not be liable for any loss or damage allegedly arising from any information or suggestion in this book.

The Oldways 4-Week Vegetarian & Vegan Diet Menu Plan

"Interest in following a plant-based diet is at an all-time high, whether people pack their plates with vegetables once a day, once a week, or all their lives. Yet there is more to vegetarian or vegan eating than just giving up meat. This book of menus, plus the Oldways Vegetarian & Vegan Diet Pyramid and other tools, will help answer questions and provide people of all ages with a well-planned and well-balanced way to enjoy vegetarian or vegan diets."

~ Sara Baer-Sinnott, President, Oldways

As Oldways decades-long exploration of the health benefits of traditional diets reinforces, many variations of vegetarian diets have existed in different cultures throughout history. The traditional vegetarian diet, illustrated in the original Oldways Vegetarian Diet Pyramid (1997) and now depicted in the updated Vegetarian & Vegan Diet Pyramid (shown on the cover of this book and on page 2), reflects the abundance of delicious, healthy foods such as vegetables, fruits, nuts, seeds, whole grains, legumes, herbs, and spices that fit into a healthy eating pattern across many different cultures. This book addresses the important nutrient-rich plant foods of the pyramid that can be eaten every day. It has been designed to serve as a guide for both health-care professionals and consumers who recognize the healthfulness of moving meat from the center of the plate and want to follow a well-balanced plant-based diet.

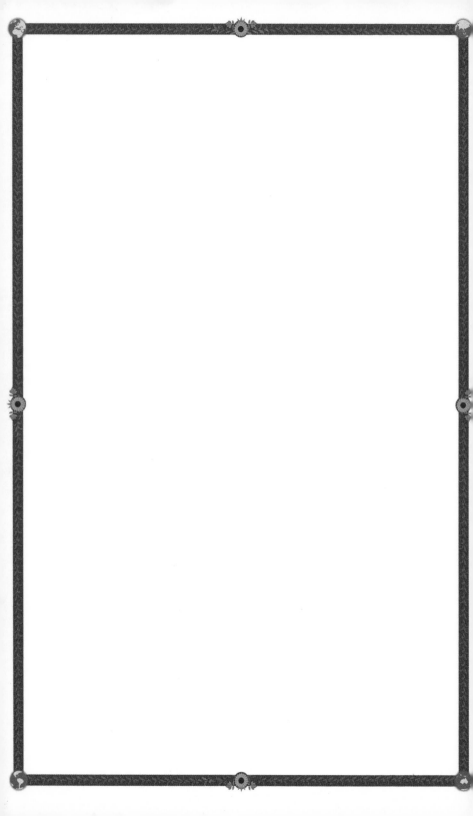

Contents

INTRODUCTION

OLDWAYS 4-WEEK MENU PLAN

NUTRITION INFORMATION

Vegetarian & Vegan Diet Pyramid

Options For Vegetarians:
Eggs and/or Dairy
including Yogurt,
Cheese, Cottage Cheese

Drink Water

Herbs, Spices, Plant Oils

Eat these
foods
every
day

Nuts, Peanuts, Seeds,
Peanut/Nut Butters

TOFU   Beans

Beans, Peas, Lentils, Soy

Whole Grains including Rice,
Barley, Millet, Oats, Quinoa,
Bread, Cereal, Pasta

Fruits and Vegetables

Be physically
active.
Cook and
share meals
with family
and friends.

Illustration by George Middleton   © 2013 Oldways Preservation and Exchange Trust   www.oldwayspt.org

The **Oldways Vegetarian & Vegan Diet Pyramid** is your tool to planning a wholesome plant-based eating style from the bottom (most important!) to the top. It's particularly important for vegetarians and vegans to plan their diets well in order to meet all of their nutritional needs for optimal health.

The **Oldways Vegetarian & Vegan Diet Servings Guide** (shown on the next page) can help balance your vegetarian or vegan diet. Choose fewer servings if you are older or less active, and more servings if you are younger and more active. To ensure that you enjoy the benefits of a nutrient-rich diet it's extremely important to eat a wide variety of plant foods – whole grains, legumes, beans, fruits, vegetables, nuts, and seeds. You may want to consult with a registered dietitian to help individualize an eating plan that meets your particular needs.

In addition, it's especially important for vegetarians and vegans to ensure that they get good sources of the following nutrients:

- **Calcium.** Eat two to three servings of calcium-rich foods every day. These include milk, cottage cheese, yogurt, and cheese, and/or calcium-rich tofu, or plant-based milk (soy, almond), kale, broccoli, dried beans, and almonds.

- **Vitamin D.** Get adequate vitamin D through exposure to the sun (about 15 to 30 minutes per day), vitamin-D fortified foods (i.e., milk for vegetarians and soymilk for vegans), and/or a vitamin D supplement (discuss with your physician).

- **Vitamin B12.** This essential nutrient is primarily available through animal foods. Vegetarians may get it in eggs and dairy products; it's recommended that vegans take a B12 supplement daily and vegetarians a few times per week.

Oldways Vegetarian & Vegan Diet Servings Guide

Foods	What counts as a serving?	Number of daily servings
Fruits	½ cup fresh, canned, or frozen fruit ¼ cup dried fruit	3–4
Vegetables	½ cup cooked or 1 cup raw vegetables	4–6
Whole Grains	1 slice whole grain bread 1 cup whole grain cereal ½ cup cooked brown rice, pasta, or other whole grains	5–8
Beans, Peas, Lentils, Soy	½ cup cooked beans, peas, or lentils ½ cup tofu 1 cup soy milk	3–6
Nuts, Peanuts, Seeds, Peanut/Nut Butters	Approx. ¼ cup nuts or seeds 2 tablespoons peanut or nut butter	1–3
Herbs, Spices, Plant Oils	Fresh or dried herbs and spices 1 teaspoon extra-virgin olive oil, canola oil, or other plant oil	Herbs/Spices: Use liberally Plant Oils: up to 5
Eggs and/or Dairy	1 egg 1 cup milk or yogurt ¼ cup cheese ½ cup cottage cheese	Eggs: 4–6 per week Dairy: 1–3

Source: Oldways Vegetarian Network Scientific Advisory Committee

8 Simple Steps

A plant-based diet can be an optimal eating style – promoting good health and a long life – if you make every bite count and keep highly processed foods to a bare minimum. By focusing on minimally processed, whole plant foods – whole grains, legumes, vegetables, fruits, nuts, seeds – you'll reap the rewards of this healthful way of eating.

The menus on the following pages are built upon these 8 simple steps:

1. Fuel Up with Healthful Protein Sources.

The majority of your protein choices should include whole food sources, including beans, lentils, soy, nuts, and seeds. Add milk, cheese, cottage cheese, and eggs if you're a vegetarian. And don't forget to enjoy minimally processed plant proteins, such as soymilk, tofu and tempeh (made from soy), and seitan (made from wheat).

2. Boost Whole Grains.

Power up on whole grains, which are naturally rich in many important nutrients, such as fiber, protein, and iron. Cook grains, such as barley, oats, quinoa, and brown, red, or black rice, and favor products made with whole grain flours.

3. Fill Your Plate with Veggies.

Include at least one or two servings of nutrient-rich vegetables – fresh, frozen, or canned – at meals and snacks throughout the day. Vegetables provide a rich supply of vitamins, minerals, phytochemicals, and even protein.

4. Make Fruit Your Daily Dessert.

You'll have no problem getting your daily servings of fruit if you enjoy it as your sweet reward after lunch and dinner. Whether it's fresh, frozen, canned, or dried, enjoy the delicious, naturally sweet taste of fruit to boost your intake of important vitamins, minerals, fiber, and phytochemicals.

5. Focus on Healthy Fats.

Don't be afraid of fats; just be selective! Healthy plant fats, including avocados, nuts, seeds, olives, (and oils made from these foods), can be a delicious and heart-healthy addition to your diet.

6. Be Picky about Beverages.

Don't waste your time (and calories) on sugary, low-nutrient beverages. Instead, quench your thirst with water and nature's plant-based beverages – coffee and tea.

7. Eat Regular, Balanced Meals.

In order to meet your daily nutritional needs, include a healthful protein source, such as beans, lentils, nuts, and tofu (and milk, cottage cheese, cheese, or eggs for vegetarians) at every meal. Balance protein with a serving of whole grains, fruits, vegetables (try to include at breakfast, too), and healthy fats, such as a drizzle of extra-virgin olive oil or a few avocado slices.

8. Make Variety Your Motto.

It's very important to eat a variety of plant foods in order to meet all of your nutritional needs. Each plant food has its own nutritional strengths, so if you combine them well over the course of a day or even a week, you'll make the most of your diet. Try to "paint" your plate with all of the colors of the rainbow – green, yellow, orange, red, purple, blue, even white and black – for maximum nutritional diversity.

Get Ready, Get Set, Cook

The most healthful – and delicious – way to follow a plant-based diet is to get into the kitchen and cook. By preparing your own meals, you can be more selective about the ingredients that go into them. Vegetarian cooking is easy! Some of the best dishes can be whipped up in mere minutes. And you don't need to be an experienced cook to pull off delicious, plant-based meals; read on to learn about the essentials that you'll need to master simple, vegetarian dishes.

Cooking Basics

Use our recipes as a guide; feel free to substitute other ingredients, such as grains, beans, vegetables, spices, and herbs, according to your preferences. And remember, you can make adjustments to these recipes as you wish.

Here are a few simple cooking techniques that we will refer to throughout these pages:

Boiling or Steaming: Many recipes call for cooking the ingredients in a pot with liquid, such as beans, whole grains, and soups. Place the necessary ingredients in the correct size pot, cover it (if the recipe calls for this), and turn the heat on. Most recipes will do fine on the medium setting.

Sautéing or Stir-frying: Most vegetable dishes can be cooked in a skillet or sauté pan (a shallow pan with straight sides). Heat a small amount of olive oil in the pan over medium heat and add the ingredients, as directed in the recipe, stirring frequently until ingredients are tender but still crisp.

Baking: Some things, such as casseroles and baked goods, develop the best flavor and texture when cooked in the oven. Place the ingredients in an ovenproof dish or pan and bake as directed – 350°F will work fine for most dishes.

Equipment List

While you don't need to invest a lot of money in equipping your kitchen for cooking, these essentials will help you create delicious, vegetarian meals:

- Can opener
- Cutting board
- Food processor, blender, or immersion blender
- Grater
- Knives (paring knife, utility knife, chef's knife)
- Measuring cups
- Measuring spoons
- Mixing bowls (small, medium, and large)
- Mixing spoon
- Pots (small, medium, and large) with lids to fit each
- Saucepan with lid
- Skillet (large)
- Spatula
- Strainer
- Vegetable peeler
- Whisk

Stocking Your Pantry

Cooking vegetarian meals is easy if you keep important shelf-stable foods on hand at all times. Here are examples of some key ingredients:

Seasonings
- Basil
- Black pepper
- Cinnamon
- Cumin
- Ginger
- Garlic
- Honey or agave nectar
- Oregano
- Salt (look for flavors, too, such as hickory smoked salt)
- Reduced-sodium soy sauce or tamari
- Turmeric
- Vinegar (mirin, rice vinegar, balsamic, and others)

Oils
- Canola oil
- Extra-virgin olive oil
- Peanut oil
- Sesame oil

Grains and Legumes
- Black beans (dried and/ or canned)
- Black-eyed peas (dried and/or canned)
- Brown rice
- Bulgur
- Cannellini beans (dried and/or canned)
- Chickpeas (dried and/ or canned)
- Farro
- Kidney beans (dried and/or canned)
- Lentils, dried
- Oats
- Quinoa
- White beans (dried and/or canned)
- White whole grain flour
- Whole grain flour
- Whole grain pasta

Nuts and Seeds
- Almonds
- Cashews
- Chia seeds
- Flaxseeds
- Hazelnuts
- Hemp seeds
- Nut and seed butters
- Peanuts and peanut butter
- Pecans
- Pistachios
- Pumpkin seeds
- Sunflower seeds
- Walnuts

Fruits and Vegetables
- Canned fruit
- Canned vegetables
- Dried fruit
- Onions
- Potatoes
- Tomato paste

Freezer List

Keep a few important foods in your freezer, too.

- Frozen fruit
- Frozen vegetables

Refrigerator List

If you keep your pantry and freezer well stocked, you can turn out wholesome meals by adding a few fresh items from your refrigerator each week.

- Cheese (dairy or plant-based)
- Cottage cheese (omit if you are vegan)
- Eggs (omit if you are vegan)
- Fresh, seasonal fruit
- Fresh, seasonal vegetables
- Milk (dairy or plant-based)
- Seitan
- Tempeh
- Tofu
- Whole grain bread
- Yogurt (dairy or plant-based)

Substitute Ingredients

We've included a range of plant-based ingredients in our menus to inspire you to explore new flavors and textures. Some of these items may not be available in your store or may cost more than staples. Here are some substitutes that we recommend:

Original Ingredient	Perfectly Good Substitute
Asiago or Pecorino cheese	Parmesan cheese (plant-based or dairy)
Black beans, red beans, white beans, chickpeas, lentils	Any type of bean, lentil, or dried pea
Bok choy	Spinach and other greens
Chia or hemp seeds	Flaxseeds
Coconut milk	Almond or soy milk
Egg	1 tbsp chia seeds or flaxseeds with 3 tbsp water=1 egg in baking
Flatbread or biscuits	Whole grain bread
Forbidden or red rice	Brown rice
Fresh fruit (i.e., kiwi, melon, berries)	Seasonal fresh, canned, or frozen fruit
Hazelnut, sunflower seed, or almond butter	Peanut butter
Fresh herbs	Dried herbs (⅓ of fresh amount)
Kale, arugula, or herb-lettuce blend	Any lettuce blend, baby spinach
Olives – Greek, Kalamata, or black	Any olives
Quinoa, farro, teff	Oats, brown rice
Seitan	Tofu
Tempeh	Tofu
Spaghetti, penne, farfalle	Any pasta shape

How to Use These Menus

The menus you'll find on the following pages are designed to help get you started on creating a healthy, nutritionally balanced vegetarian or vegan lifestyle. At Oldways, our focus is on traditional foods and meals made with wholesome, real ingredients. In fact, many countries around the world celebrate plant-based foods, from the Middle East's hummus to Latin America's salsa verde, Africa's tubers and greens, and Asia's stir-fries. You will find a world of delicious, healthy foods awaiting you in the next four weeks.

- **Mix and match.** Take a breakfast from one day's menu, lunch from another, and dinner or dessert from a third day. You may find a favorite breakfast that you'd like to repeat every day, or a dinner you want to cook every week. Let your taste preferences be your guide, and remember that this is not a rigid plan. Add in your favorite whole grains or vegetables as you wish.

- **Each day's menu totals about 1,500 – 1,600 calories.** For most people, this level will produce a slow, healthful weight loss. However, if you're already at a healthy weight, you can add some extra servings. Check out our "Extras" in the Bonus Pages section for snacks and additions.

- **What about dairy?** The menu plans do not call for dairy or plant-based milk specifically, but we encourage you to add 2–3 servings of these into your meal plan every day, as you see fit, in order to meet your protein, calcium and vitamin D needs.

- **All of our recipes are healthful and nutritious.** When you combine them in a balanced diet with plenty of additional fruits and vegetables, as guided by the Vegetarian & Vegan Diet Pyramid (see page 2), you will meet all of your nutritional needs. However, we recommend that vegetarians and vegans supplement their diets with vitamin B12 (100% RDA), and get adequate calcium (found in calcium-rich plant-based milk and tofu and green vegetables) and vitamin D (found in vitamin-D fortified plant-based milk, UV-treated mushrooms, as well as exposure to the sun). If you're interested in learning about the nutritional information for our recipes and foods, see page 78.

Breakfast 1-2-3 Plan

A Healthy Start

The best breakfasts include all of the major food groups on the Vegetarian & Vegan Diet Pyramid (see page 2) – whole grains, fruits, vegetables, and protein-rich foods like dairy, soymilk, nuts, and beans. Use this 1-2-3 plan to build your own healthy breakfast plan, choosing one item from each category every day. See page 3 for serving sizes.

❶ Whole Grains

Pick one of these delicious, whole grain choices:

- Bagel
- Bread
- Cereal
- English muffin
- Grits
- Muffin
- Oatmeal
- Pancake or waffle
- Pita bread
- Quinoa porridge
- Toast
- Tortilla (i.e., whole wheat, corn)
- Wheat berry porridge

❷ Fruits and/or Vegetables

Pick one or two delicious fruits and vegetables as part of your breakfast. Add fruits to your cereal or eat on the side; use vegetables as a topping or filling for whole grain bread, pita bread, or a tortilla, or eat on the side. Here are some of our favorites:

Fruits
- Apple or applesauce
- Banana
- Berries
- Cherries
- Grapefruit
- Grapes
- Melon
- Orange
- Peach
- Pear
- Pineapple
- Raisins

Vegetables
- Arugula or lettuce leaves
- Sliced avocado
- Sautéed or uncooked bell pepper
- Sautéed or uncooked mushrooms
- Sautéed onion
- Sliced radishes
- Sautéed or uncooked spinach
- Sliced or baked tomato

❸ Protein

Pick a serving from this category to accompany your whole grain serving, or to eat on the side.

Dairy and plant-based alternatives
- Cheese
- Cottage cheese
- Milk (reduced-fat)
- Soymilk
- Yogurt

Eggs (omit if you are vegan)

Hummus

Legumes
- Beans
- Chickpeas
- Lentils
- Peas
- Soybeans

Nuts and Seeds
- Almonds
- Almond butter
- Cashews
- Chia seeds
- Flaxseeds (ground)
- Hemp seeds
- Peanut butter
- Peanuts
- Pecans
- Pistachios
- Pumpkin seeds
- Sunflower seeds
- Tahini
- Walnuts

Tofu

● Drink water with your meal and coffee or tea, if you wish.

Weekends

On the days that you're not rushed, invest a bit more time in baking or making a special breakfast. Consider one of these choices:

- **Vegetable Breakfast Hash** (page 30)
- **Banana-Walnut Bread** (page 49)
- **Cottage Cheese Pancakes** (page 57)

Whole Grain Cereals

When it comes to whole grain porridges, think beyond oatmeal. Many cultures enjoy simmered whole grains, such as teff or millet, for breakfast. Try quinoa, brown rice, wheat berries, or rye berries, for an interesting – and healthful – twist. Better yet, enjoy leftover whole grains from the night before, or cook up a whole pot and reheat portions during the week. (You can also freeze leftover portions in sealed plastic bags to reheat out of the bag in the microwave.) Top with fruit, milk or plant-based milk, and nuts or seeds and you've got a wholesome breakfast that will stick with you all morning.

Lunch Ideas

For lunch, we've offered you two choices each day – either a simple, creative meal idea, or the suggestion to use leftovers saved from your week of plant-based eating. The lunch menus include sandwiches, salads, soups, stews, and wraps. We've included recipes where we thought they'd be helpful. Some come with easy instructions, while others have simple recipes. If you'd like to venture from the menu, just swap one of these basic lunches for any other day of the week.

5 Steps to a Fabulous Salad

1. Mound fresh salad greens – such as kale, romaine, iceberg, arugula, or butter leaf lettuce – on your plate.

2. Add some of your favorite vegetables, such as sliced or diced carrots, tomatoes, artichoke hearts, bell peppers, broccoli, or asparagus. Or, add sliced fruit including mangoes, papayas, peaches, or pears, or dried fruit such as raisins, cranberries, or blueberries.

3. Add a protein source, such as a sliced hard-boiled egg, cottage cheese, cheese, baked tofu, beans, sunflower seeds, or almonds.

4. Sprinkle on a serving of whole grains, such as cooked whole grain pasta, quinoa, or red, black, or brown rice. Or, include a serving of whole grain bread on the side.

5. Add a drizzle of dressing. Good choices include extra-virgin olive oil, and/or flavored vinegar. Or, make your own (see page 70).

Check out some of our favorite salads:

- **Farro–Cabbage Salad** (page 37)
- **Rice Tabbouleh Salad** (page 43)
- **Barley with White Beans** (page 51)

How to Make Tasty Sandwiches or Wraps

A good old-fashioned sandwich can be the perfect solution for a quick and easy lunch.

1. Choose a good whole grain bread (look for the Whole Grain Stamp as the sign of a wholesome choice, page 72).

2. Spread with your favorite healthy sandwich spread, such as pesto, hummus, tahini, peanut or nut butter, or mashed avocado.

3. Top with plenty of vegetables, including lettuce, basil, arugula, tomatoes, avocados, cucumbers, sprouts, and bell peppers.

4. Add a protein source, such as baked tofu or seitan and/or cheese.

5. Think beyond "ordinary" bread. Try whole grain wraps, tortillas, or flat bread. Here are some of our favorite sandwiches to get you started:

- **Pita Bread with Hummus and Vegetables** (page 15)
- **Veggie Wrap** (page 25)
- **Grilled Cheese Sandwich with Tomato and Avocado** (page 48)

Soups, Stews, and Chili

The most comforting – and wholesome – meals often start with a bowl of soup, stew, or chili. By pairing a vegetable soup with your sandwich or salad, you will round out your meal and at the same time add an important serving of vegetables. Or, choose a hearty main-dish stew or chili – starring beans, lentils, peas, vegetables, and/or whole grains – to form the base of your entire meal. Here are some easy and affordable recipes that you can rely on each week:

- **Camelback Chili** (page 23)
- **League of Nations Lentil Soup** (page 31)
- **Minestrone** (page 53)

Traditional Appeal

One of the easiest and most delicious ways to enjoy plant-based meals is to include more traditional, ethnic dishes. Most cultures around the world, from Mediterranean and Indian to Asian, Middle Eastern, and African, have wonderful, traditional dishes based on plants. Try some of these exotic lunch ideas:

- **Black Bean Avocado Quesadilla** (page 26)
- **Manhattan Millet Cakes** (page 31)
- **Fattoush** (page 61)

Love Those Leftovers!

The simplest lunch of all calls on leftovers from dinner the night before. After all, why do all that cooking for just one meal? Most of our recipes make about four servings. If you're cooking for more than four, double the batch so that you end up with delicious food for the next day or two. Place leftovers in an airtight container; you can store them in the refrigerator for up to three days. The next day you can take them to work to reheat in a microwaveable dish. Bon appetit!

Day 1

Breakfast ① whole grains ② fruit/vegetables ③ protein

①③ 2 slices whole grain toast with 2 tablespoons almond butter

② 1 orange

Chai tea (optional milk, dairy or plant-based)

Lunch

Pita Bread with Hummus and Vegetables

6–8 ounces plain yogurt (dairy or plant-based) with
½ cup sliced peaches and 1 tablespoon ground flaxseeds

Iced tea

Dinner

Vegetable Stir-Fry 101 with Rice

½ cup grapes

Lemon mineral water

Tip

Rely on a Rice Cooker
Not only can you make easy, fluffy rice with a rice cooker, it's great for cooking up any whole grain, such as farro, wheat berries, or quinoa. Just add grains and water (according to the package directions), push the button, and walk away.

Recipes

Pita Bread with Hummus and Vegetables   Serves 1

Experiment with the many different flavors of hummus you can find at your grocery store.

1 whole wheat pita bread, sliced in half
Lettuce
4 cucumber slices

4 tomato slices
4 Kalamata olives
4 avocado slices
4 tablespoons hummus

Fill each pita bread half with lettuce, cucumber, tomato, olives, and avocado. Top with hummus. Serve immediately or pack for a meal away from home.

Vegetable Stir-Fry 101 with Rice   Serves 4

Master this basic recipe so you can always whip up a delicious meal in minutes.

1 tablespoon sesame oil
1 medium onion, sliced
1 medium carrot, sliced
1 red bell pepper, sliced
1 yellow bell pepper, sliced
5-6 large mushrooms, sliced
2 cloves garlic, minced
1 teaspoon minced gingerroot

1 8-ounce package extra-firm tofu, drained and cubed
¼ teaspoon red pepper flakes
2 tablespoons reduced-sodium soy sauce
2 tablespoons orange juice
2 cups sliced baby bok choy
2 cups cooked brown rice (cooked according to package directions)

Heat the olive oil in a large skillet or saucepan and sauté the onion, carrot, and pepper over medium-high heat for 4 minutes, stirring occasionally. Add the mushrooms, garlic, gingerroot, and tofu, and cook for an additional 4 minutes. Add the red pepper flakes, soy sauce, orange juice, and bok choy and sauté for an additional 2–5 minutes, until the greens are cooked. Serve over brown rice.

Day 2

Breakfast ① whole grains ② fruit/vegetables ③ protein

① ② ½ whole grain English muffin with 2 avocado slices

② ½ cup berries

③ **Scrambled Eggs with Cottage Cheese and Herbs** (or ½ cup baked tofu)

Coffee (optional milk, dairy or plant-based)

Lunch

Veggie Club Sandwich: 2 slices whole grain bread, layered with cheese (dairy or plant-based) lettuce, tomato slices, bell pepper slices, and pickles

OR Leftovers: Reheat **Vegetable Stir-Fry 101 with Rice** from Day 1 dinner.

½ cup unsweetened applesauce

Mineral water

Dinner

Sweet Potato Curry with Millet

1 pear, sliced in wedges, with 2 tablespoons cashew butter

Mint tea

Tip

Love Your Bones!
Every day, power up on bone-building foods such as calcium-rich milk, cottage cheese, yogurt, soymilk and tofu (fortified with calcium), green leafy vegetables, and almonds.

Recipes

Scrambled Eggs with Cottage Cheese and Herbs   Serves 2

If you don't eat eggs, substitute crumbled tofu for the first three ingredients.

2 large eggs
¼ cup low-fat cottage cheese
1 tablespoon milk
½ teaspoon Italian seasoning

1 teaspoon extra-virgin olive oil
Salt and freshly ground pepper to taste

Combine the eggs, cottage cheese, milk, and seasonings in a small mixing bowl and blend with a fork. Heat the olive oil in a small skillet. Pour in the egg mixture, and cook, stirring occasionally, until the eggs are firm and cooked through. Season with salt and pepper.

Sweet Potato Curry with Millet   Serves 6

This is an easy dish to make ahead and simply reheat a night or two later. Try serving it with other grains, such as brown rice, bulgur, farro, or quinoa.

1 tablespoon extra-virgin olive oil
1 medium onion, diced
3 cloves garlic, minced
1 red bell pepper, diced
2 carrots, diced
1 stalk celery, diced
1 tablespoon curry powder
1 teaspoon cardamom
1 teaspoon cinnamon
½ teaspoon ginger

1 large sweet potato, peeled and diced
1 14.5-ounce can diced tomatoes, with juice
1 15-ounce can chickpeas, drained, rinsed
⅓ cup light coconut milk
½ cup roasted unsalted peanuts
½ cup raisins
3 cups cooked millet (cooked according to package directions)

Heat the olive oil in a large saucepan over medium heat. Add the onion and garlic and sauté for 5 minutes, or until soft. Add the pepper, carrots, and celery, and cook for 5 minutes. Stir in the curry powder, cardamom, cinnamon, and ginger, and cook for 3 minutes. Add the sweet potato, tomatoes, chickpeas, and coconut milk and cook for 2 minutes. Cover, reduce the heat to medium-low, and simmer for 15 to 20 minutes, until the sweet potato is fork-tender. Stir in the peanuts and raisins, remove from the heat, and let sit, covered, for 5 minutes. Serve hot, with millet.

Day 3

Breakfast ① whole grains ② fruit/vegetables ③ protein

①②③ 1 cup oatmeal with 1 chopped baked apple, ¼ cup chopped almonds, and 1 cup dairy or plant-based milk

Coffee (optional milk, dairy or plant-based)

Lunch

Beet Salad

1 cup tomato-lentil soup

3-4 (1 ounce) whole grain crackers

OR Leftovers: Reheat **Sweet Potato Curry with Millet** from Day 2 dinner

1 small banana

Dinner

Farfalle with Avocado Sauce

1 cup spinach salad with ½ cup cannellini beans, 1 tablespoon pistachios, and **Herb Vinaigrette** (page 70)

½ cup grapes

Café latte (dairy or plant-based milk)

Tip

Shake Up Some Dressing
Make your own simple, delicious vinaigrette with just a few ingredients in a jar with a tight-fitting lid. (See page 70 for some easy recipes.)

Beet Salad   Serves 6

Use a combination of yellow and red beets to add extra color. Cook them separately.

4 cups salad greens
2 cups chopped, cooked beets (cooled)
½ cup chopped dates
½ cup walnuts
Balsamic Vinaigrette (page 70)

Combine the salad greens, beets, dates, and walnuts in a salad bowl. Pour the vinaigrette over the salad, toss, and serve.

Farfalle with Avocado Sauce   Serves 6

Penne also goes nicely with this delicious, creamy sauce. Add up to ½ cup of chopped fresh basil or parsley if you wish.

1 14.5-ounce package whole grain farfalle (cooked according to package directions)
2 cloves garlic, chopped
1 tablespoon extra-virgin olive oil
Juice of 1 lemon
2 ripe avocados, peeled and pitted, or 1 cup guacamole
6 cherry tomatoes, halved
¼ teaspoon crushed red pepper
Salt and freshly ground pepper to taste
Parmesan cheese (dairy or plant-based, optional)

Cook the farfalle. While the pasta is cooking, combine the garlic, olive oil, and lemon juice in a food processor. Add the avocados, tomatoes, and red pepper and blend until smooth. Season with salt and pepper. Garnish with cheese.

Day 4

Breakfast ① whole grains ② fruit/vegetables ③ protein

①②③ 2 4-inch whole grain waffles (frozen or from mix) with 1 tablespoon maple syrup, ½ cup blueberries, and 2 tablespoons ground flaxseeds

Coffee (optional milk, dairy or plant-based)

Lunch

1 cup split pea soup

3-4 (1 oz) whole grain crackers

French Potato Salad

OR Leftovers: Reheat **Farfalle with Avocado Sauce** from Day 3 dinner.

½ cup fresh or frozen cherries

Iced tea

Dinner

Lentils with Sriracha Sauce

½ cup cooked barley

1 cup tossed green salad with ½ cup cherry tomatoes, 1 tablespoon pine nuts, and **Balsamic Vinaigrette** (page 70)

½ cup pineapple chunks

Coffee

Tip

Wholesome Canned or Packaged Soups

Some canned or packaged soups contain almost half your daily limit of sodium (2,300 milligrams per day) in a single serving. Read the labels to find soups that contain less than 400 mg per serving. Buy those made with real, wholesome ingredients, such as legumes, grains, vegetables, herbs, and spices.

French Potato Salad   Serves 4

The secret to this delicious salad is adding the dressing while the potatoes are still warm.

6 yellow potatoes
2 tablespoons extra-virgin olive oil
1 tablespoon Dijon mustard
¼ cup chopped fresh tarragon
   (or 1 tablespoon dried)

Salt and freshly ground pepper
   to taste
2 cups chopped romaine lettuce

Cook the potatoes in a large pot of boiling water until tender. Drain and cool slightly. Combine the olive oil and mustard in a mixing bowl. When cool enough to handle but still warm, chop the potatoes and add them to the dressing, along with the tarragon and salt and pepper. Serve at room temperature on a bed of lettuce.

Lentils with Sriracha Sauce   Serves 4

Mix the cooked lentils with mashed potatoes for true comfort food.

1 cup uncooked lentils
1 tablespoon extra-virgin olive oil
1 onion, chopped
1 cup mushrooms, chopped
1 clove garlic, minced
½ cup finely chopped walnuts
1 cup whole grain breadcrumbs

1 tablespoon lemon juice
1 tablespoon reduced-sodium soy
   sauce
Salt and black pepper to taste
½ teaspoon turmeric
Sriracha sauce, to taste

Combine the lentils and 2 cups of water in a saucepan, bring just to a boil, reduce the heat to medium-low and cook for about 30 minutes, until tender. Drain and set aside. Preheat the oven to 350°F. Heat the oil in a large skillet and sauté the onion, mushrooms, and garlic over medium-low heat, for about 8 minutes. Add the cooked lentils, walnuts, breadcrumbs, lemon juice, soy sauce, and seasonings and sauté for 3 minutes. Transfer the mixture to a lightly greased, 6-cup baking dish and bake for 30 minutes. Serve warm, topped with Sriracha sauce.

Day 5

Breakfast ① whole grains ② fruit/vegetables ③ protein

① ② ③ **Breakfast Burrito:** 1 large whole grain tortilla (whole wheat or corn), ½ cup diced tomatoes, bell peppers, and onions, 2 tablespoons salsa, ½ cup refried black beans, 2 tablespoons shredded cheese (dairy or plant-based)

② ½ cup blueberries

Coffee (optional milk, dairy or plant-based)

Lunch

Camelback Chili

1 small slice cornbread

OR Leftovers: Reheat **Lentils with Sriracha Sauce** from Day 4 dinner, or serve as a sandwich filling in a whole grain pita bread half.

Carrot and Cabbage Slaw: Blend 1 cup shredded carrots and cabbage with 1 tablespoon sesame seeds and **Honey-Mustard Vinaigrette** (page 70)

½ cup raspberries, fresh or frozen

Iced tea

Dinner

Pasta with Kale

½ cup apricots

Café latte (dairy or plant-based milk)

Tip

Quick & Easy Veggies

If chopping fresh vegetables is too time consuming on your busiest days, try some of the pre-chopped fresh varieties available in your supermarket produce section, including grated carrot and slaw mixes, sliced onions and bell peppers, and pre-washed salad greens. These are also a great help if you suffer from arthritis.

Recipes

Camelback Chili   Serves 4

You can also use canned beans. See note below.

1 cup uncooked kidney beans
1 yellow onion, diced
2 tablespoons chopped chilies in
   adobo sauce
2 cloves garlic, minced
½ tablespoon maple syrup

½ teaspoon red pepper flakes
1 teaspoon chili powder
½ teaspoon turmeric
½ teaspoon cumin
Sea salt or hickory-smoked salt
   to taste

Soak the beans overnight in enough water to cover. Drain and add to a pot with 3 cups of water and all the remaining ingredients. Bring just to a boil over high heat, reduce the heat to medium-low, cover, and cook for 1 hour, or until the beans are tender. Check several times as the beans cook, and add a bit more water if necessary to keep them from drying out.

Note: In a hurry? Open two cans of beans, drain and rinse them. Heat 1 tablespoon of olive oil in a large skillet, add the remaining ingredients, and sauté until the onions are soft. Add the beans, and cook until heated through.

Pasta with Kale   Serves 4

Substitute Swiss chard or spinach for the kale in this greens-based pesto.

8 ounces whole grain pasta
1 tablespoon extra-virgin olive oil
1 onion, diced
3 cloves garlic
1½ teaspoons dried oregano
1 8-ounce container extra-firm
   tofu, cubed

Salt and black pepper to taste
4 cups chopped kale
½ cup pine nuts or coarsely
   chopped walnuts

Cook the pasta in a large pot of boiling water, according to package directions. Drain and cover to keep warm. Heat the olive oil in a large sauté pan, add the onion, garlic, oregano, and tofu, season with salt and pepper, and sauté for 2 minutes. Add the kale, cover, and cook, stirring occasionally, until the kale is just wilted, but still bright green, about 4 minutes. Add the kale to the pasta and toss lightly. Sprinkle with the pine nuts and serve warm.

Day 6

Breakfast ❶ whole grains ❷ fruit/vegetables ❸ protein

❶❷❸ **Grits with Scrambled Egg and Tomato Slices:** 1 cup cooked whole grain grits, 4 tomato slices, 1 scrambled egg (or ½ cup baked, cubed tofu)

❷ 1 orange

Coffee (optional milk, dairy or plant-based)

Lunch

Tomato soup (1 cup)

Veggie Wrap

OR Leftovers: Reheat **Camelback Chili** from Day 5 dinner and garnish with chopped lettuce and tomatoes, avocado slices, tortilla strips, and scallions for a delicious taco salad.

1 kiwi

Green tea

Dinner

Oat Risotto with Fava Beans and Asparagus

1 cup spinach salad with sliced mushrooms and **Balsamic Vinaigrette** (page 70)

1 apple

Iced tea

Tip

Pantry Essential: Canned Beans
Beans – rich in protein and powerful nutrients – should be an essential part of your plant-based eating style. Stock a variety of canned (low-salt or no salt added) beans in your pantry to add to salads, pasta dishes, casseroles, and soups.

Recipes

Veggie Wrap   Serves 1

This also makes an easy, quick dinner on a busy night.

1 whole grain wrap
½ cup diced extra-firm tofu
¼ cup sprouts
2 tablespoons chopped scallions
2 tablespoons fresh cilantro
2 tablespoons chopped cucumber

2 tablespoons sliced bell pepper
¼ cup mandarin oranges
1 tablespoon chopped almonds
1 tablespoon **Sesame Vinaigrette**
(page 70)

Lay the wrap out on a work surface. Arrange the tofu, sprouts, vegetables, oranges, and almonds in the center of the wrap. Drizzle with the vinaigrette. Roll up burrito-style. Slice in half or in 1-inch pieces.

Oat Risotto with Fava Beans and Asparagus   Serves 4

Risotto is traditionally made with Arborio rice, but oats are a budget-friendly, delicious substitute.

3 cups reduced-sodium vegetable
   broth
½ cup white wine
1 tablespoon extra-virgin olive oil
1 onion, diced
2 cloves garlic, minced

1 bunch (12 ounces) fresh
   asparagus, trimmed and chopped
1 15-ounce can fava beans, drained
   and rinsed
Pinch freshly ground black pepper
1 cup uncooked steel-cut oats
1 teaspoon dried oregano

Heat the broth and wine in a saucepan until warm but not boiling. Keep warm over very low heat. Heat the olive oil in a large saucepan. Add the onion and garlic and sauté for 3 minutes. Add the asparagus, beans, and black pepper and sauté for 1 minute. Stir the oats and oregano into the vegetable mixture. Ladle ½ cup of the hot broth into the oat mixture. Cook, stirring constantly, until the liquid is absorbed, adding additional small amounts of broth when the oat mixture begins to look dry, until all the broth is incorporated and the risotto is creamy and tender, about 20 minutes. Serve hot.

Day 7

Breakfast ① whole grains ② fruit/vegetables ③ protein

①② 1 **Bran-Raisin Muffin**

② ½ cup orange juice

②③ ½ cup cottage cheese (or ½ cup cubed, baked tofu) with 2 tomato slices

Coffee (optional milk, dairy or plant-based)

Lunch

1 cup vegetable soup

Black Bean Avocado Quesadilla: 1 small corn tortilla with ¼ cup black beans, ¼ cup shredded cheese (dairy or plant-based), topped with another corn tortilla. Microwave 2 minutes and top with ¼ sliced avocado and ¼ cup salsa.

OR Leftovers: Reheat **Oat Risotto with Fava Beans and Asparagus** from Day 6 dinner.

½ cup mango chunks

Passion fruit iced tea

Dinner

Spicy Thai Noodles

1 cup cucumbers with mint and 1 tablespoon sesame seeds

½ Asian pear

Iced green tea

Tip

What Is Seitan?
Available in many supermarkets today, seitan is a traditional Asian food made from the protein (gluten) of wheat. Nutritious and protein-rich, seitan has a mild taste and "meaty" texture and is excellent in stir-fries, curry dishes, and casseroles.

Recipe

Bran-Raisin Muffins   Makes 12

Serve leftovers with apple butter and/or nut butter.

1½ cups white whole wheat flour
½ cup oat bran
2 teaspoons baking powder
1 teaspoon cinnamon
½ teaspoon ginger
¼ teaspoon salt
¼ cup vegetable oil

2 tablespoons brown sugar
1 egg (or 1 tablespoon ground chia seeds mixed with 3 tablespoons water)
1 cup milk (dairy or plant-based)
1 cup raisins

Preheat the oven to 400°F. Spray a 12-cup muffin pan with non-stick cooking spray. Combine the flour, oat bran, baking powder, cinnamon, ginger, and salt in a mixing bowl and blend with a whisk. In a second bowl combine the oil, brown sugar, egg, and milk and whisk until smooth. Add the wet ingredients to the dry ingredients and stir just until blended. Fold in the raisins. Spoon the batter into the muffin-pan cups, filling them half full with batter, and bake for 15 to 20 minutes. Let cool slightly before removing from the pan.

Spicy Thai Noodles   Serves 4

No need to rely on takeout when you master this easy recipe.

8 ounces Asian brown rice noodles
1 teaspoon peanut oil
1 tablespoon vegetarian Thai chili paste
2 cloves garlic, minced
½ teaspoon minced gingerroot
½ teaspoon coriander
½ teaspoon cumin
½ teaspoon cinnamon

1 cup canned light coconut milk
1 cup sliced mushrooms
1 8-ounce package seitan, sliced
2 tablespoons reduced-sodium soy sauce
¾ cup diced scallions
6 ounces baby bok choy, trimmed, leaves separated
½ cup chopped peanuts

Cook the rice noodles in boiling water, according to the package directions. Drain, rinse, and set aside. Heat the peanut oil in a large skillet over medium heat. Add the chili paste, garlic, gingerroot, coriander, cumin, cinnamon, coconut milk, mushrooms, seitan, and soy sauce, and sauté for 4 minutes. Add the noodles and scallions and stir well. Place the bok choy leaves on top, cover, and cook for 4 minutes longer. Garnish with chopped peanuts.

Day 8

Breakfast ① whole grains ② fruit/vegetables ③ protein

① 1 small whole grain muffin

② ③ **Breakfast Smoothie**

Jasmine tea

Lunch

Baked Tofu Sandwich with Sprouts and Tomatoes: Spread 2 slices whole grain bread with 2 tablespoons hummus, add ½ cup baked tofu, ½ cup sprouts, and 2 tomato slices.

1 cup green salad with **Honey Mustard Vinaigrette** (page 70)

OR Leftovers: Reheat **Spicy Thai Noodles** from Day 7 dinner.

½ cup trail mix: ¼ cup raw nuts and ¼ cup dried fruit

Cinnamon spice tea

Dinner

Southwestern Beans and Rice

1 cup sautéed greens

1 peach

Iced tea with lemon

Tip

Whip Up a Smoothie
Whether it's for breakfast or a snack, a well-planned smoothie can deliver powerful nutrients and flavor. Include dairy or plant-based milk (or cottage cheese or yogurt), fruit, vegetables, and nuts or seeds.

Recipes

Breakfast Smoothie   Serves 1

Enjoy for breakfast or make ahead and take to work for your lunch.

½ cup frozen berries (strawberries, raspberries, blackberries, blueberries)
¼ cup orange juice
½ cup milk (dairy or plant-based)
2 tablespoons ground flaxseeds
¼ cup old-fashioned oats
½ teaspoon vanilla

Place all ingredients in a large blender container and process until smooth.

Southwestern Beans and Rice   Serves 4

Add 1 cup chopped tempeh for the last 20 minutes of cooking time,
if you wish.

1 cup uncooked kidney beans
1 carrot, sliced
1 onion, sliced
1 bay leaf
¼ teaspoon black pepper
¼ teaspoon cayenne pepper
½ teaspoon dried cilantro
1 cube or 2 teaspoons vegetable bouillon
2 cups cooked long-grain brown rice (cooked according to package
   directions)
Chopped fresh cilantro for garnish (optional)

Soak the beans overnight in water to cover. Drain and combine in a large
pot with 2 cups of water, carrots, onion, bay leaf, black pepper, cayenne
pepper, cilantro, and bouillon. Stir well, bring just to a boil, reduce the heat
to medium-low, cover, and cook until the beans are soft, about 1 hour and
45 minutes. Garnish with cilantro and serve with brown rice.

Day 9

Breakfast ❶ whole grains ❷ fruit/vegetables ❸ protein

❶ 1 slice whole grain toast

❷ ❸ **Vegetable Breakfast Hash**: Sauté ½ cup chopped tofu or 1 egg with 1 cup chopped vegetables and ½ cup shredded potatoes and serve with mashed avocado, guacamole, or salsa.

❷ ½ cup cranberry juice

Coffee (optional milk, dairy or plant-based)

Lunch

League of Nations Lentil Soup

3-4 (1 oz) whole grain crackers

OR Leftovers: Reheat **Southwestern Beans and Rice** from Day 8 dinner.

1 cup **Vegetable Confetti Salad**: Toss lettuce greens with colorful diced or shredded fresh vegetables and **Honey-Mustard Vinaigrette** (page 70)

1 banana with 2 tablespoons peanut butter

Iced jasmine tea

Dinner

Manhattan Millet Cakes

½ cup mashed root vegetables (potatoes, turnips, carrots, celery root, rutabaga, and/or parsnips)

½ cup cooked Brussels sprouts with ½ cup tempeh and **Sesame Vinaigrette** (page 70)

1 orange

Coffee

Tip

Spice It Up!
Don't forget about the power of herbs and spices to flavor foods, as well as give them an antioxidant and anti-inflammatory health kick. Get into the habit of using liberal quantities of fresh, chopped herbs in salads, soups, stews, and pasta dishes.

League of Nations Lentil Soup   Serves 6

Try other greens, such as Swiss chard or kale, in this easy soup.

1 tablespoon extra-virgin olive oil
1 onion, chopped
2 carrots, chopped
2 stalks celery, chopped
2 cloves garlic, minced
1 teaspoon curry powder
6 cups reduced-sodium vegetable broth

1 cup uncooked lentils
1 14.5-ounce can diced tomatoes, with juice
2 cups baby spinach (optional)
Parmesan cheese (dairy or plant-based, optional)

Heat the olive oil in a large pot over medium heat. Add the onion, carrots, celery, and garlic, and sauté for 5 minutes. Add the curry powder and cook for 1 minute. Add the broth and lentils and cook, uncovered, over medium heat for 30 minutes, until the lentils are soft but not mushy. Add the tomatoes with their juice and the spinach, if using, and simmer for 10 minutes. Serve with Parmesan cheese, if you wish.

Manhattan Millet Cakes   Makes 6

Serve hot, on a bed of mixed greens, topped with mustard, guacamole, and/or edamame hummus.

1 cup uncooked millet
10 chopped sun-dried tomatoes
1 clove garlic, minced
⅓ cup pitted green olives, chopped
¼ cup raw sunflower seeds
¼ cup packed grated Pecorino or Parmesan cheese (or plant-based cheese)

1 tablespoon capers, rinsed, drained, and minced
2 teaspoons dried oregano
1 tablespoon extra-virgin olive oil
3 cups mixed salad greens
Mustard

Combine the millet and 3 cups of water in a pot and bring to a boil. Reduce the heat to medium-low, cover, and simmer for 30 minutes. Drain if necessary and transfer the millet to a bowl. When cool, add the sun-dried tomatoes, garlic, olives, sunflower seeds, cheese, capers, and oregano. Stir well, mashing the ingredients together. Use dampened hands to form 6 patties. Heat the olive oil in a large skillet and cook the patties until lightly brown and crisp, about 4 minutes on each side. Serve on a bed of greens with the mustard.

Day 10

Breakfast ① whole grains ② fruit/vegetables ③ protein

① ③ 2 small whole grain cinnamon-flax pancakes (Use a mix and stir in cinnamon and 2 tablespoons chia or flaxseeds.)

② ½ cup applesauce

③ 1 cup hot chocolate (made with dairy or soymilk)

Lunch

1 cup miso-vegetable soup

Thai Peanut Wrap

OR Leftovers: Reheat **Manhattan Millet Cakes** from Day 9 dinner and serve with cheese (dairy or plant-based), lettuce, tomatoes, and a dollop of hummus or guacamole.

½ cup sliced pineapple

Iced green tea with lemon

Dinner

Vegetable Couscous

1 cup green bean salad with 1 tablespoon almonds and **Herb Vinaigrette** (page 70)

3 figs (fresh or dried)

Mint tea

Tip

Chia vs. Eggs
Chia seeds are packed with healthy fats, protein, and fiber, and they also can replace eggs in baking. Just mix 1 tablespoon ground chia seeds with 3 tablespoons water to form a gel to replace one egg in a recipe.

Recipes

Thai Peanut Wrap
Serves 1

You can omit the tortilla and enjoy this tasty filling on a bed of salad greens.

1 cup broccoli slaw mix
1 tablespoon chopped scallion
½ cup cubed tempeh
1 tablespoon chopped peanuts
1 tablespoon **Thai Vinaigrette** (page 70)
1 whole grain tortilla

Combine the broccoli slaw mix, scallion, tempeh, peanuts, and vinaigrette in a bowl. Lay the tortilla out on a work surface, spoon the filling into the center, and roll, burrito-style.

Vegetable Couscous
Serves 6

This full-bodied stew is also delicious with rice.

1 tablespoon extra-virgin olive oil
1 clove garlic, minced
1 onion, chopped
2 sweet potatoes, peeled and cubed
2 carrots, sliced
1 eggplant, diced
3 tablespoons harissa
1 teaspoon each: cumin, cardamom, coriander, turmeric
1 14.5-ounce can diced tomatoes, with juice
1 15-ounce can chickpeas, drained and rinsed
1½ cups reduced-sodium vegetable broth
3 cups cooked whole wheat couscous (cooked according to package directions)

Heat the olive oil in a large saucepan, add the garlic, onion, sweet potatoes, carrots, and eggplant, and sauté for 10 minutes, stirring occasionally. Add the harissa, spices, tomatoes, chickpeas, and broth. Cover, and simmer for about 45 minutes, until the vegetables are tender. Spoon ½ cup of cooked couscous into serving bowls and top with the hot stew.

Day 11

Breakfast ① whole grains ② fruit/vegetables ③ protein

①②③ **Breakfast Sandwich:** 2 slices whole grain toast, 1 hard-boiled egg (or 2 tablespoons tahini), 1 ounce cheese (dairy or plant-based), 2 tomato slices and 2 avocado slices

② 1 orange

Black tea (optional milk, dairy or plant-based)

Lunch

1 cup gazpacho

3–4 (1 ounce) whole grain crackers

Curried Red Quinoa and Peach Salad

OR Leftovers: Reheat **Vegetable Couscous** from Day 10 dinner.

Dinner

Enchilada Casserole

1 cup sautéed zucchini with 2 tablespoons walnuts

½ cup papaya slices

Tip

How to Sauté Vegetables

To serve delicious vegetables, try sautéing them. It's easy! Just add a drizzle of olive oil to a hot skillet, along with chopped fresh vegetables, and your favorite herbs and spices, and cook, stirring occasionally, for a few minutes, until the vegetables are tender but still crisp.

Curried Red Quinoa and Peach Salad   Serves 4

Instead of peaches, try diced mango or pineapple in this salad. It's a guaranteed hit for a buffet table.

1 cup uncooked red quinoa
Pinch of salt
1 15-ounce can white beans, drained and rinsed
2 peaches, peeled and diced (or canned, drained)
4 scallions, minced
½ cup minced fresh cilantro or parsley

3 tablespoons vanilla soy or almond yogurt
Juice of 1 lemon
1 tablespoon extra-virgin olive oil
1 teaspoon curry powder
½ cup slivered almonds
8 cups salad greens

Rinse the quinoa and add to a pot with 2 cups of water and salt. Bring just to a boil, reduce the heat to medium-low, cover, and cook for 15 minutes. Set aside, covered, for 10 minutes. Fluff with a fork and transfer to a large bowl to cool. When cool, add the beans, peaches, scallions, and cilantro and toss gently. In a small bowl combine the yogurt, lemon juice, olive oil, curry powder, and blend with a whisk until smooth. Pour the dressing over the salad and toss to combine. Garnish with the almonds and pile onto a bed of salad greens. Serve at room temperature.

Enchilada Casserole   Serves 6

Get your kids to help you make this easy, yummy dinner.

1 10-ounce can green enchilada sauce
6 whole grain tortillas
1 15-ounce can reduced-sodium black beans, drained and rinsed
1 tomato, diced

2 cups packed baby spinach leaves
1 cup frozen corn, thawed
5 scallions, chopped
⅓ cup chopped fresh cilantro
1½ cups shredded cheese (dairy or plant-based)

Preheat the oven to 375°F. Cover the bottom of a large baking dish with some of the enchilada sauce. Assemble the enchiladas on a flat work surface. Down the center of each tortilla, arrange about ⅓ cup beans, 1 tablespoon tomato, ⅓ cup spinach, 3 tablespoons corn, 2 tablespoons scallions, and 1 tablespoon cilantro. Roll up tightly, burrito style, and place each enchilada, seam side down, on top of the sauce in the baking dish. Cover with the remaining enchilada sauce and sprinkle with the cheese and remaining scallions. Bake uncovered for 35 minutes, until golden brown.

Day 12

Breakfast ① whole grains ② fruit/vegetables ③ protein

① ③ 1 small toasted whole grain bagel with 2 tablespoons hazelnut spread

② ½ grapefruit

White tea

Lunch

Farro-Cabbage Salad

1 cup navy bean-vegetable soup

OR Leftovers: Reheat **Enchilada Casserole** from
Day 11 dinner.

½ cup grapes

Chai tea

Dinner

Pasta Pomodoro

1 cup cooked lima and green bean blend

½ cup cantaloupe chunks

Cafe latte (dairy or plant-based milk)

Tip

Adopting Whole Grain Pasta
Using whole grain pasta is a great way to add more whole grains
to your diet. However, it may take a bit of time to get used to its
nutty chewiness. Start with 51% whole grain pasta, and choose
shapes, such as penne or rotini, in order to become accustomed
to the taste and texture of whole grain.

Recipes

Farro-Cabbage Salad   Serves 4

For a different flavor, substitute packaged broccoli slaw for the cabbage.

2½ cups shredded cabbage (red or white)

2 cups cooked farro (cooked according to package directions)

3 scallions, sliced

½ cup chopped fresh parsley

3 tablespoons orange juice

1½ tablespoons extra-virgin olive oil

1 clove garlic, minced

¼ teaspoon red chili pepper flakes

½ teaspoon cumin

½ teaspoon chili powder

¼ teaspoon turmeric

In a large bowl, toss together the cabbage, farro, scallions, and parsley. In a small bowl, whisk together the orange juice, olive oil, garlic, red pepper flakes, cumin, chili powder, and turmeric. Pour the dressing on the salad, toss, and serve.

Pasta Pomodoro   Serves 8

Smoked paprika gives the sauce for this dish a sweet-spicy flavor, but feel free to omit it if you don't have any on hand.

1 tablespoon extra-virgin olive oil

1 small onion, diced

3 cloves garlic, minced

1 28-ounce can diced tomatoes, with juice

¼ teaspoon smoked paprika

1 14-ounce package whole grain pasta

Salt and freshly ground pepper to taste

½ cup fresh basil leaves, chopped or 1 teaspoon dried

1 cup Parmesan or plant-based cheese

½ cup pine nuts or chopped walnuts

Heat the olive oil in a large skillet. Add the onion and garlic and sauté for about 8 minutes over medium-low heat. Place the canned tomatoes in a blender and pulse for 2-3 seconds, to create a thick sauce. Add the sauce and smoked paprika to the onion mixture. Cook just until bubbly. Season as desired with salt and pepper, and keep the sauce warm over low heat. Bring a large pot of water to a boil. Add the pasta and cook according to package directions. Place the drained, hot pasta on a serving platter, top with the sauce, fresh basil leaves, cheese, and pine nuts, and serve.

Day 13

Breakfast ❶ whole grains ❷ fruit/vegetables ❸ protein

❶❷❸ 1 cup cooked steel-cut oats with 1 sliced banana, ¼ cup peanuts, and 1 cup dairy or plant-based milk

Coffee (optional milk, dairy or plant-based)

Lunch

Vegetable-Bean Stew

1 slice whole grain French bread

OR Leftovers: Reheat **Pasta Pomodoro** from Day 12 dinner.

½ cup apricots

Lavender tea

Dinner

Quick Coconut Curry with Rice

Endive salad with 1 cup beets, 2 tablespoons almonds and **Vinaigrette** (page 70)

Sesame crackers (1 oz)

1 pear

Iced green tea

Tip

Discover Slow-Cooker Magic

A slow cooker can be your ally in following a plant-based diet. It's an easy solution for brewing your own vegetable stock or cooking up delicious stew and chili featuring whole grains and legumes. Simply add the ingredients and turn the dial; 4 to 6 hours on high or 8 to 10 hours on low should do it for most recipes.

Recipes

Vegetable-Bean Stew   Serves 8

If you don't have time to soak and cook dry beans, use 2 cans of drained, rinsed beans instead. Cut the water back to 3 cups and simmer all ingredients for about 30 minutes, or until the vegetables are tender.

1½ cups uncooked beans (kidney, pinto, etc.)
1 15-ounce can diced tomatoes, with juice
1 onion, chopped
3 carrots, chopped
3 celery stalks, coarsely chopped
1 bell pepper, sliced
3 red potatoes, peeled and cubed

1 cube or 1 teaspoon vegetable bouillon
2 teaspoons dried tarragon
1 bay leaf
3 cloves garlic, minced
½ teaspoon celery salt
Salt and freshly ground pepper to taste

Soak the beans in water to cover overnight. Drain and place in a pot with 5 cups of water and the remaining ingredients. Stir well, bring just to a boil, reduce the heat to medium-low, cover, and cook for about 2 hours, until tender. Season as desired with salt and pepper.

Quick Coconut Curry with Rice   Serves 4

Substitute extra-firm tofu for the seitan and experiment with frozen vegetable blends to create different flavors.

1 tablespoon sesame oil
1 teaspoon grated gingerroot
1 clove garlic, minced
1 teaspoon curry powder
½ teaspoon red pepper flakes
½ cup reduced-sodium vegetable broth
1 small head cauliflower, chopped

1 14.5-ounce can diced tomatoes, with juice
1½ cups frozen peas, thawed
1 8-ounce package seitan, diced
½ cup light coconut milk
2 cups cooked brown rice (cooked according to package directions)

Heat the oil in a large saucepan, add the gingerroot, garlic, curry powder, and Aleppo pepper, and cook over medium heat for 2 minutes. Add 1 cup of water, the broth, cauliflower, and tomatoes, and stir well. Bring to a boil, reduce the heat to medium-low, cover, and simmer for 10 minutes. Add the peas, seitan, and coconut milk, cover, and cook for 5 minutes longer. Serve with brown rice.

Day 14

Breakfast ① whole grains ② fruit/vegetables ③ protein

① ③ **Huevos Rancheros:** 1 fried egg or ½ cup refried pinto beans with 1 small corn tortilla and 2 tablespoons salsa

② 1 clementine

Coffee (optional milk, dairy or plant-based)

Lunch

Vietnamese Noodle Soup

1 cup bok choy salad with **Sesame Vinaigrette** (page 70)

OR Leftovers: Reheat **Quick Coconut Curry with Rice** from Day 13 dinner.

½ cup mixed fruit

Red tea

Dinner

Bean Burger with whole grain bun, lettuce, 2 tomato slices, 1 ounce cheese (dairy or plant-based) and 2 tablespoons guacamole

½ cup sautéed California blend vegetables with 2 tablespoons almonds

1 apple

Iced peach tea

Tip

Cooking Up Veggie Burgers
While homemade veggie burgers are usually your healthiest and tastiest option, you may want to keep a few frozen products on hand for easy meal solutions. Look for those that are moderate in sodium and contain ingredients you can find in a home kitchen. Serve on whole grain buns.

Recipes

Vietnamese Noodle Soup   Serves 4

This fragrant soup is especially delicious the day after you make it.

4 cups reduced-sodium vegetable broth
1 yellow onion, chopped
½ cup sliced mushrooms
1 carrot, sliced
1 stalk lemongrass, peeled and minced
1 teaspoon minced gingerroot
1 tablespoon reduced-sodium soy sauce
1 tablespoon rice wine vinegar
¼ teaspoon ground black pepper
2 tablespoons chopped fresh basil
2 tablespoons chopped fresh cilantro
1 8-ounce package flat rice noodles
1 8-ounce package tofu, diced
1 cup fresh bean sprouts
4 scallions, sliced

Combine the broth, onion, mushrooms, carrot, lemongrass, gingerroot, soy sauce, vinegar, black pepper, basil, and cilantro in a large pot. Bring just to a boil, reduce the heat to medium-low, cover, and simmer for 30 minutes. Cook the noodles according to package directions, drain, and rinse with hot water. Add the noodles to the broth along with the tofu, bean sprouts, and scallions. Heat for 2 minutes and serve hot, in bowls.

Bean Burgers   Serves 6

Allow at least 4 hours for the mixture to chill before you shape the burgers. Otherwise, the mixture will be very sticky. Serve plain or in whole grain buns, with lettuce, sliced tomatoes, and guacamole.

2 tablespoons extra-virgin olive oil
1 onion, chopped
1 carrot, chopped
2 cloves garlic (or more to taste), minced
1 egg (or 1 tablespoon ground chia seeds in 3 tablespoons water)
1 15-ounce can pinto beans, drained and rinsed, or 2 cups cooked beans
½ cup chopped walnuts
1 cup whole grain bread crumbs
1 cup cooked brown rice

Heat 1 tablespoon of the olive oil in a large skillet over medium heat. Add the onion, carrot, and garlic and cook, stirring occasionally, for about 5 minutes, until the onion is soft. Transfer the mixture to a food processor. Add the egg, beans, and walnuts and pulse once or twice, to make a coarse mixture. Put the mixture into a mixing bowl and stir in the bread crumbs and rice. Cover with plastic wrap and chill. When ready to cook, remove the burger mixture from the refrigerator and form into eight patties. Heat the remaining 1 tablespoon of olive oil in the frying pan over medium-high heat. Brown the patties in batches for 6 to 8 minutes on each side. Serve hot.

Day 15

Breakfast ❶ whole grains ❷ fruit/vegetables ❸ protein

❶ 1 slice whole grain toast with 1 tablespoon jam or fruit spread

❷ ½ cup orange juice

❷ ❸ **Veggie Mushroom Omelet:** ½ cup chopped vegetables and mushrooms cooked with 1 egg or ½ cup shredded tofu, and 1 ounce cheese (dairy or plant-based)

English breakfast tea (optional milk, dairy or plant-based)

Lunch

Rice Tabbouleh Salad

¼ cup **Hummus** (page 70)

½ whole wheat pita bread

1 ounce feta cheese or 6 ounces soy yogurt

OR Leftovers: Reheat a **Bean Burger** from Day 14 dinner and enjoy in a whole grain bun with lettuce and tomato slices.

½ cup raisin/pumpkin-seed blend

Cafe au lait (dairy or plant-based)

Dinner

Shepherds Pie

1 cup baby spinach salad with **Balsamic Vinaigrette** (page 70)

Whole grain dinner roll

1 watermelon wedge

Raspberry Iced tea

Tip

Get Your Greens!
Green leafy vegetables – kale, spinach, Swiss chard, collards, romaine, and beyond – are nutrition power-houses! Not only are they packed with dozens of essential vitamins, minerals, and phytochemicals, many are also rich in plant-based calcium.

Rice Tabbouleh Salad   Serves 6

Traditionally made with bulgur wheat, this popular summer salad is also delicious made with rice. Try it with barley or farro, too.

3 cups cooked brown rice (cooked according to package directions)

1 cup chopped, Italian flat-leaf parsley

¾ cup chopped cucumber

¾ cup chopped tomato

¼ cup minced mint leaves

2 tablespoons extra-virgin olive oil

¼ cup lemon juice

Pinch of salt

1 teaspoon ground black pepper

Combine all ingredients in a large bowl and toss well.

Shepherds Pie   Serves 4

The sauce in this dish is tasty enough to stand in as gravy with mashed potatoes at a holiday feast.

⅓ cup raw cashews

¼ cup uncooked traditional oats

2 tablespoons reduced-sodium soy sauce

1 tablespoon nutritional yeast

1 teaspoon curry powder

1 tablespoon extra-virgin olive oil

1 onion, diced

1 clove garlic, minced

1 teaspoon thyme

Salt and pepper to taste

1 16-ounce package frozen mixed vegetables, thawed

1 15-ounce can kidney beans, drained and rinsed

2 cups mashed potatoes (about 4 medium potatoes cooked and mashed with 2 tablespoons extra-virgin olive oil)

Preheat the oven to 375°F. Combine the cashews, oats, soy sauce, and nutritional yeast in a blender along with 2¼ cups of very hot water and blend until very smooth. Pour the mixture into a saucepan and cook over medium heat for about 4 minutes, stirring with a whisk, until the sauce thickens. Stir in the curry powder and set aside. Heat the olive oil in a large skillet and sauté the onion and garlic for 8 minutes. Add the seasonings, mixed vegetables, and kidney beans, and cook for 5 minutes. Spoon the mixture into a 2-quart baking dish, pour the sauce on top, and cover with the mashed potatoes. Bake for 30 minutes. Serve hot.

Day 16

Breakfast ① whole grains ② fruit/vegetables ③ protein

① ③ 2 small **Pumpkin-Pecan Pancakes:** Stir a spoonful of canned pumpkin and 2 tablespoons chopped pecans into whole grain pancake mix and cook as directed.

② ½ cup applesauce

Café mocha (dairy or plant-based)

Lunch

Veggie Pizza

OR Leftovers: Reheat **Shepherds Pie** from Day 15 dinner.

1 cup assorted salad greens with ½ cup chickpeas and **Herb Vinaigrette** (page 70)

½ cup blueberries with 1 tablespoon chia seeds

Cinnamon spice tea

Dinner

Stir-Fry with Noodles

1 cup Chinese cabbage slaw with **Thai Vinaigrette** (page 70)

½ cup cherries

Oolong tea

Tip

Fruit for Dessert
The best way to fit in three or more servings of fruit each day is to enjoy it as dessert. The naturally sweet flesh of fruit is packed with disease protective nutrients, too.

Recipes

Veggie Pizza
Serves 8

Mix it up by using hummus in place of the marinara sauce.

1 16-ounce package refrigerated, prepared whole wheat pizza dough

⅓ cup marinara sauce

1½ teaspoons dried oregano

1 cup grated cheese (dairy or plant-based)

1 small zucchini, sliced

1 red bell pepper, diced

1 cup mushrooms, sliced

3 scallions, sliced

⅓ cup pistachios

Preheat the oven to 350°F. Roll out the pizza dough and place it on a pizza pan or stone. Spread the marinara sauce over the dough and sprinkle with the oregano and cheese. Arrange the zucchini, bell pepper, mushrooms, scallions, and pistachios over the pizza. Bake for about 30 minutes, until cooked through. Cut into slices and serve hot.

Stir-Fry with Noodles
Serves 4

Substitute sliced bell peppers, mushrooms, and baby bok choy for any of the vegetables in this quick dish.

1 tablespoon peanut oil

1 onion, sliced

2 carrots, chopped

2 celery stalks, chopped

1 8-ounce package tempeh, cubed

1 teaspoon minced gingerroot

2 cloves garlic, minced

8 ounces snow peas

2 tablespoons reduced-sodium soy sauce

2 tablespoons orange juice

¼ teaspoon red pepper flakes

⅓ cup slivered almonds

1 8-ounce package rice noodles (cooked according to package directions)

Heat the peanut oil in a large skillet or wok and cook the onion, carrots, and celery for 8 minutes. Add the tempeh, gingerroot, garlic, and snow peas, and cook until the vegetables are tender but still crisp. Stir in the soy sauce, orange juice, red pepper flakes, almonds, and cooked rice noodles, and heat through. Serve hot or at room temperature.

Day 17

Breakfast ❶ whole grains ❷ fruit/vegetables ❸ protein

❶❷❸ 1 cup cooked teff with ¼ cup dried apricots and ¼ cup chopped walnuts

❷ ½ cup orange juice

Ceylon orange pekoe tea (optional milk, dairy or plant-based)

Lunch

1 cup vegetable soup

Williamsburg Kale Salad

1 whole grain roll with 2 tablespoons peanut butter

1 banana

Pomegranate iced tea

OR Leftovers: Reheat **Stir-Fry with Noodles** from Day 16 dinner.

Dinner

Pasta Puttanesca

1 cup three-bean medley (green beans, kidney beans, and lima beans)

1 wedge honeydew melon

Coffee (optional milk, dairy or plant-based)

Tip

Get to Know Ancient Grains
A world of ancient grains, such as teff, kamut, farro, and spelt, awaits you. These crunchy, nutty grains are packed with nutrients. Just simmer them according to package directions and serve as a breakfast cereal or side dish, or add them to salads.

Recipes

Williamsburg Kale Salad
Serves 4

If you haven't tried raw kale, this salad will introduce you to the possibilities.

1 pound kale, finely chopped
Juice of 1 whole lemon
1½ tablespoons extra-virgin olive oil
¼ teaspoon black pepper

1 teaspoon Dijon mustard
1 8-ounce package baked tofu, cubed
2 small crisp apples, sliced

Put the kale in a large salad bowl. Whisk together the lemon juice, olive oil, black pepper, and mustard. Drizzle the dressing over the kale and massage it into the leaves with clean fingers. Add the tofu and apples, toss, and serve immediately.

Pasta Puttanesca
Serves 8

This traditional recipe celebrates the spirit of Italian cooking – making "something out of nothing."

1 tablespoon extra-virgin olive oil
1 onion, diced
3 cloves garlic, minced
1 28-ounce can diced tomatoes, with juice
1 tablespoon tomato paste
3 tablespoons capers, drained
½ cup packed, pitted, and halved Italian olives

½ teaspoon dried basil
½ teaspoon red pepper flakes
1 pound whole grain spaghetti
1 cup shredded Asiago or plant-based cheese

Heat the olive oil in a large skillet and sauté the onion and garlic for 6 minutes. Add the tomatoes, tomato paste, capers, olives, basil, and red pepper flakes. Cook on low heat for 15 minutes, stirring occasionally, until the sauce thickens. Keep warm over low heat. Bring a large pot of water to a boil, add the spaghetti, and cook according to the package directions. Drain and serve topped with sauce and garnished with cheese.

Day 18

Breakfast ① whole grains ② fruit/vegetables ③ protein

① ② 1 slice **Banana-Walnut Bread**

② ½ cup raspberries

③ ½ cup cottage cheese (or soy yogurt)

Cafe au lait (dairy or plant-based)

Lunch

Grilled Cheese Sandwich with Tomato and Avocado: 2 slices whole grain bread, 2 ounces cheese (dairy or plant-based), 2 tomato slices, and 2 avocado slices

1 cup minestrone

OR Leftovers: Reheat **Pasta Puttanesca** from Day 17 dinner.

1 apple

Darjeeling tea

Dinner

Dal with Rice

1 cup cucumber-tomato salad with pine nuts

1 persimmon

Chai tea

Tips

Look for Whole Grain Breads

When you're choosing bread, make sure that you look for whole grain ingredients, such as whole wheat, oats, rye, barley, and quinoa, listed first on the label. Or look for the Whole Grain Stamp (see page 72) on the package, which indicates the product contains a good amount of whole grains.

Recipes

Banana-Walnut Bread
Serves 12

Delicious all by itself, this moist bread is also good with fruit or nut butter.

3 ripe bananas, mashed
¼ cup canola oil
⅓ cup agave nectar or honey
1 egg or 1 teaspoon egg replacer
1 teaspoon baking soda
¼ teaspoon salt

1½ cups white whole wheat flour
1 teaspoon cinnamon
⅓ cup finely chopped walnuts
⅓ cup chocolate chips (optional)

Preheat the oven to 350°F. In medium mixing bowl, combine the bananas, canola oil, agave, and egg and stir well. Add the remaining ingredients and stir just until well combined. Spray a loaf pan with non-stick cooking spray. Scrape the batter into the pan and bake for about one hour, until cooked through. Cool and remove from the pan. Let the bread sit for about one hour before slicing.

Dal with Rice
Serves 4

Serve with chutney and a green salad for an easy and tasty weeknight meal.

1 cup uncooked lentils
2 carrots, sliced
1 bell pepper, chopped
1 onion, chopped
2 red potatoes, chopped
2 tomatoes, chopped
1 teaspoon garam masala

½ teaspoon grated gingerroot
1 clove garlic, minced
¼ teaspoon red chili flakes
Salt to taste
2 cups cooked brown basmati rice
  (cooked according to package
  directions)

Combine all ingredients, except for the rice, plus 3 cups of water, in a large pot, stir well, and bring to a boil. Reduce the heat to medium-low, cover, and cook for about 45 minutes, until all the vegetables are tender. Serve with brown rice.

Day 19

Breakfast ❶ whole grains ❷ fruit/vegetables ❸ protein

❶❷❸ **Quinoa Porridge:** 1 cup cooked quinoa (cooked according to package directions) with ¼ cup chopped dried figs, ¼ cup chopped pistachios, and 1 cup dairy or plant-based milk

Café Americano (optional milk, dairy or plant-based)

Lunch

Barley with White Beans

1 slice (1 oz) whole grain flatbread

1 sliced tomato with basil and 1 tablespoon pine nuts

OR Leftovers: Reheat **Dal with Rice** from Day 18 dinner.

½ cup pineapple chunks

Lemon tea

Dinner

Pasta with Roasted Vegetables

1 cup succotash salad (corn, lima beans, diced bell pepper) with **Herb Vinaigrette** (page 70)

½ cup strawberries with ½ cup cottage cheese or plant-based yogurt

Tip

Roast Those Veggies!
Roasting vegetables in a hot oven (375° to 400° F) for 10 to 30 minutes with a drizzle of olive oil brings out their deep, sweet flavors and provides the perfect accompaniment for many foods, including sandwiches, salads, and side dishes.
Try combinations of vegetables, including asparagus, carrots, beets, peppers, sweet potatoes, squash, and onions.

Recipes

Barley with White Beans   Serves 6

Substitute baby arugula for the baby kale if you wish and try black barley, or a mix of black and white barley. You can also make this tasty salad with cooked farro, bulgur, or brown rice.

1 cup uncooked hulled barley
1 tablespoon extra-virgin olive oil
1 red onion, finely chopped
2 stalks celery, diced
2 red, orange, or yellow bell peppers, diced

Salt and pepper to taste
1 tablespoon balsamic vinegar
1 15-ounce can cannellini beans, drained and rinsed
4 cups lightly packed baby kale

Combine the barley and 3 cups of water in a medium pot over medum-high heat. Bring just to a boil, reduce the heat to medium-low, cover, and cook for 50 minutes, or until tender. Remove from the heat and set aside. Heat the olive oil in a large skillet, add the red onion, celery, and diced pepper, and sauté for about 5 minutes, until the vegetables are tender. Add the salt, peppers, and balsamic vinegar, and stir well. Stir in the beans and kale and cook for 3 to 4 minutes, until the kale is wilted and the beans are heated through. Serve warm or at room temperature.

Pasta with Roasted Vegetables   Serves 6

Experiment with yellow squash, peppers, and other vegetables.

2 zucchini, chopped
4 cups cherry tomatoes, halved
2 Asian eggplants, thinly sliced on the diagonal
2 cups sliced mushrooms
Olive oil spray
Salt and pepper to taste

1 14-ounce box whole grain farfalle
½ cup chopped fresh basil or parsley
½ cup toasted walnuts or hazelnuts
½ cup Parmesan, shredded mozzarella, or plant-based cheese (optional)

Preheat the oven to 400° F. Arrange the zucchini and tomatoes on one baking sheet, the eggplants and mushrooms on another. Spray lightly with olive oil and season to taste with salt and pepper. Roast for 20 minutes, turning once with a spatula, until the vegetables are soft and lightly browned. While the vegetables are roasting, cook the farfalle according to the package directions, drain, and return to the cooking pot. Add the roasted vegetables, basil, and walnuts. Mix gently and turn out into a large serving bowl. Serve warm, topped with cheese, if you wish.

Day 20

Breakfast ① whole grains ② fruit/vegetables ③ protein

①②③ 1 cup whole grain breakfast cereal with ¼ cup raisins,
2 tablespoons hemp seeds, and 1 cup dairy or plant-based milk

Earl Grey tea (optional milk, dairy or plant-based)

Lunch

Minestrone

1 slice whole grain Italian bread

OR Leftovers: Reheat **Pasta with Roasted Vegetables** from Day 19 dinner.

1 cup green salad with 2 tablespoons sunflower seeds and
Balsamic Vinaigrette (page 70)

6 ounces yogurt (dairy or soy) with ½ cup kiwi slices and ¼ cup granola

Café latte (dairy or plant-based)

Dinner

Sonoma Vegetable Kebabs with Spelt

1 cup carrot-pineapple-bulgur slaw tossed
with **Sesame Vinaigrette** (page 70)

1 orange

Iced berry tea

Tip

Get to Know Tofu
Tofu is a nutrient-rich staple that complements any vegetarian
diet. It comes in a variety of textures, ranging from soft to extra
firm. Use softer tofu for blending into dips, smoothies, or fillings;
use firmer tofu in entrees, such as stir-fries, or for kebabs.

Recipes

Minestrone
Serves 8

This easy soup always tastes better the second day. Add a spoonful of pesto at the end of the cooking time to ramp up the flavor.

3 cups reduced-sodium vegetable broth

1 28-ounce can diced tomatoes, with juice

1 15-ounce can cannellini or kidney beans, drained and rinsed

2 celery stalks, diced

1 onion, diced

1 zucchini, sliced

1 red potato, cubed

1 carrot, sliced

2 cloves garlic, minced

1 tablespoon Italian seasoning blend

2 cups packed, chopped Swiss chard or spinach

1 tablespoon acini de pepe or other tiny pasta shape

Parmesan cheese (dairy or plant-based, optional)

Combine all ingredients (except for the spinach, pasta, and Parmesan) in a large pot, bring just to a boil, reduce the heat to medium-low, cover, and simmer for 45 minutes. Add the spinach and pasta and cook for an additional 10 minutes. Serve hot, garnished with cheese.

Sonoma Vegetable Kebabs with Spelt
Serves 4

Slide leftovers off the skewers with a fork and serve them as a taco filling.

1 15-ounce package extra-firm tofu, cut into large cubes

1 onion, cut into wedges

1 bell pepper, cut into wedges

1 summer squash, cut into wedges

4 ounces large whole mushrooms

2 tablespoons extra-virgin olive oil

3 tablespoons lemon juice

1 teaspoon rosemary

1 clove garlic, minced

¼ teaspoon black pepper

Salt to taste

2 cups cooked spelt (cooked according to package directions)

Thread the tofu and vegetable wedges onto 4 skewers and arrange in a shallow dish. Whisk together the olive oil, lemon juice, rosemary, garlic, black pepper, and salt (if using). Drizzle the marinade over the skewers, turn each skewer to coat well, and chill for 1 hour. Cook the kebabs over a hot grill for about 10 minutes on each side; or oven broil them about 8 inches from the heat for about 10 minutes on each side; or bake them in a 400°F oven for about 15 minutes on each side. Serve with spelt.

Day 21

Breakfast ① whole grains ② fruit/vegetables ③ protein

① ③ 1 cup old-fashioned oatmeal, ¼ cup chopped almonds, and 1 cup dairy or plant-based milk

② ½ cup berries

Coffee (optional milk, dairy or plant-based)

Lunch

1 cup tomato soup

Quinoa-Spinach Salad

3-4 (1 oz) whole grain crackers with 2 tablespoons peanut butter

OR Leftovers: Reheat **Sonoma Vegetable Kebabs with Spelt** from Day 20 dinner.

½ pomegranate

Oolong tea

Dinner

Farmers Market Lasagna

1 cup arugula salad with ½ cup chickpeas and **Herb Vinaigrette** (page 70)

1 slice whole grain garlic bread

1 wedge cantaloupe

Café au lait (dairy or plant-based)

Tip

Make Vegetarian Versions of Family Favorites
One of the best ways to introduce delicious, vegetarian meals into your life is to convert classics, such as lasagna, chili, or tacos. Just replace the meat with a plant-based ingredient, such as beans or tofu.

Recipes

Quinoa-Spinach Salad   Serves 4

Use any other kind of beans and experiment with other whole grains, such as barley, bulgur, farro, or freekeh, in place of the quinoa.

1 15-ounce can black beans, drained and rinsed

2 cups cooked quinoa (cooked according to package directions)

¼ cup finely chopped red onion

3 cups packed baby spinach

1 lemon, juiced

1½ tablespoons extra-virgin olive oil

1 clove garlic, minced

½ teaspoon cumin

¼ teaspoon paprika

¼ cup pine nuts

Combine the beans, quinoa, onion, and spinach in a mixing bowl. Whisk together the lemon juice, olive oil, garlic, cumin, and paprika in a small bowl. Drizzle the dressing over the salad and toss. Garnish with pine nuts and serve.

Farmers Market Lasagna   Serves 8

Buy the freshest vegetables you can find to bring summertime flavor to this family favorite, which always tastes best the second day.

1 tablespoon extra-virgin olive oil

1 onion, chopped

1 bell pepper, chopped

1 zucchini, sliced

1½ cups chopped broccoli

2 cloves garlic, minced

½ teaspoon ground black pepper

2 teaspoons oregano

4 ounces (6 sheets) whole grain lasagna noodles, uncooked

1 24-ounce jar marinara sauce

2 cups packed, chopped greens (mustard, kale, spinach)

1½ cups shredded cheese (dairy or plant-based)

Preheat the oven to 375°F. Heat the olive oil in a large skillet, add the onion, bell pepper, zucchini, broccoli, garlic, black pepper, and oregano, and sauté for about 7 minutes. In a deep baking dish, layer 3 lasagna noodles, half of the vegetable mixture, 1 cup of greens, half of the marinara sauce, and half of the cheese. Repeat the layers, cover, and bake for 1 hour. Remove the cover and bake for an additional 15 minutes.

Day 22

Breakfast ① whole grains ② fruit/vegetables ③ protein

① ② ③ **Cottage Cheese or Vegan Pancakes** with ½ cup peach slices

② ½ cup vegetable juice

Coffee (optional milk, dairy or plant-based)

Lunch

Black Bean Burrito: 1 large whole grain tortilla, ½ cup black beans, ½ cup assorted vegetables, 2 tablespoons salsa, and ¼ cup cheese (dairy or plant-based)

OR Leftovers: Reheat **Farmers Market Lasagna** from Day 21 dinner.

1 cup carrot sticks with 2 tablespoons almond butter

½ cup mixed fruit

Mango iced tea

Dinner

Black-Eyed Peas with Rice and Plantains

1 cup cooked greens with sesame seeds

1 small slice cornbread

1 wedge watermelon

Café au lait (dairy or plant-based)

Tip

Wrap It Up!
One of the easiest veggie meals comes wrapped up in a whole grain tortilla. Fill it with your favorite toppings, including beans, lettuce, greens, chopped veggies, avocado slices or guacamole, cheese (dairy or plant-based), nuts, tofu, tempeh, hummus, vinaigrette, dried fruit, and/or salsa.

Recipes

Cottage Cheese Pancakes   Serves 4

Here's a great weekend treat. Add a bit more milk if the batter seems too thick.

1 cup white whole wheat flour
½ teaspoon baking soda
1 teaspoon baking powder
2 tablespoons ground flaxseeds
1 tablespoon brown sugar
Pinch of salt

3 eggs
1 cup (8 ounces) small-curd
    cottage cheese
1 ripe banana, mashed
¾ cup milk (dairy or plant-based)
1 tablespoon canola oil

Combine the flour, baking soda, baking powder, flaxseeds, brown sugar, and salt in a mixing bowl and blend with a whisk. In a second bowl combine the eggs, cottage cheese, banana, milk, and oil and whisk until smooth. Using a large spoon, stir the wet ingredients into the flour mixture, just until the batter is smooth. Heat a griddle sprayed with nonstick cooking spray. Using a ¼ cup measure for each pancake, drop the batter onto the hot griddle and cook until golden brown on each side.

Vegan Pancakes: Combine 2 tablespoons ground flaxseeds and 3 tablespoons water in a small bowl and set aside. Add 1 tablespoon apple cider vinegar to 1¼ cups soy milk in a second bowl and set aside. Combine 1 cup white whole wheat flour, 1½ teaspoons baking powder, 1 tablespoon brown sugar, and ½ teaspoon salt in a bowl and blend with a whisk. Add the wet ingredients to the dry ingredients and stir just until smooth.

Black-Eyed Peas with Rice and Plantains   Serves 4

Plantains, which look like bananas, are very easy to cook. Boil them for about 5 minutes, or until the seams split open, peel, and cut into chunks.

1 tablespoon extra-virgin olive oil
1 onion, diced
1 red or orange bell pepper, diced
2 cloves garlic, minced
1 teaspoon grated gingerroot
1 tablespoon curry powder
½ cup light coconut milk
1 tablespoon honey or agave nectar

Juice from 1 lime
1 15-ounce can black-eyed peas
Salt and freshly ground pepper to
    taste
2 cups cooked brown rice (cooked
    according to package directions)
2 plantains, cooked and sliced

Heat the olive oil in a large saucepan, add the onion, garlic, and pepper, and sauté for about 4 minutes, until soft. Add the gingerroot and curry powder and cook for 2 minutes more. Stir in the coconut milk along with ½ cup of water, the honey, and the lime juice and stir until smooth. Add the peas, cover, and cook for 10 minutes. Serve with brown rice and plantains.

Day 23

Breakfast ❶ whole grains ❷ fruit/vegetables ❸ protein

❶ 1 slice whole grain toast with 1 tablespoon jam or fruit spread

❷ ½ cup home fries (potatoes sautéed with bell peppers and onions)

❷ ½ cup grapefruit juice

❸ 1 fried egg (or ½ cup baked tofu)

Breakfast tea (optional milk, dairy or plant-based)

Lunch

Barley-Vegetable Soup

1½ cups Greek salad (lettuce, tomatoes, cucumbers, 1 ounce feta cheese or plant-based cheese) and **Vinaigrette** (page 70)

1 slice whole grain flat bread

OR Leftovers: Reheat **Black-Eyed Peas with Rice and Plantains** from Day 22 dinner.

½ cup trail mix: ¼ cup nuts and ¼ cup dried fruit

Mint iced tea

Dinner

Asian Peanut Stir-Fry with Black Rice

1 cup mache salad with **Vinaigrette** (page 70)

½ cup mango slices

Green tea

Tip

What Is Tempeh?
Tempeh is a traditional fermented soy and grain-based food that originated in Indonesia. Available in most grocery stores today, it can be easily chopped or crumbled into stir-fries, wraps, salads, and casseroles. You can also steam it for 5-10 minutes and toss it with your favorite marinade.

Recipes

Barley-Vegetable Soup   Serves 8

Enjoy this hearty soup for lunch or dinner. Substitute brown rice or farro for the barley, and test for doneness after about 40 minutes.

1 14.5-ounce can diced tomatoes, with juice

1 15-ounce can cannellini beans, drained and rinsed

2 cubes or 2 teaspoons reduced-sodium vegetable bouillion

2 cloves garlic, minced

1 cup uncooked barley

2 carrots, sliced

2 stalks celery, sliced

1 cup sliced leeks

1 cup sliced mushrooms

1 teaspoon marjoram

Dash of black pepper

Sea salt to taste

Combine all the ingredients with 5 cups of water in a large pot, stir well, and bring just to a boil. Reduce the heat to medium-low, cover, and simmer for about 1 hour. Serve hot.

Asian Peanut Stir-Fry with Black Rice   Serves 4

Brown rice is fine for a quick dinner, but the lovely color of black rice will make this dish extra special.

1 tablespoon peanut oil

1 onion, sliced

2 cloves garlic, minced

1 16-ounce package frozen Asian vegetable blend, thawed

1 8-ounce package tempeh, cubed

1 teaspoon minced gingerroot

2 tablespoons reduced-sodium soy sauce

1 teaspoon Thai red curry paste

1/3 cup peanuts, chopped

2 cups cooked black rice (cooked according to package instructions)

Heat the peanut oil in a large skillet or wok. Add the onion and garlic and cook for about 8 minutes. Add the vegetable blend, tempeh, and gingerroot and cook, stirring frequently, until the vegetables are tender but still crisp. Stir in the soy sauce, curry paste, and peanuts and heat through. Serve hot, with black rice.

Day 24

Breakfast ❶ whole grains ❷ fruit/vegetables ❸ protein

❶❸ 2 slices toasted whole grain baguette with 2 tablespoons peanut butter

❷ 1 orange

Hot chocolate (dairy or plant-based)

Lunch

Fattoush

1 cup lentil soup

OR Leftovers: Reheat **Asian Peanut Stir-Fry with Black Rice** from Day 23 dinner.

1 large date

White tea

Dinner

Pasta with Spinach

1 cup broccoli slaw with **Herb Vinaigrette** (page 70)

½ cup berries

Coffee (optional milk, dairy or plant-based)

Tip

Go Med!
One of the most widely researched diets on the planet is the delicious Mediterranean Diet, which has been linked to a number of health benefits. This eating style also happens to be plant-based, offering great inspiration for vegetarians. Visit oldwayspt.org for more information on the Mediterranean Diet.

Recipes

Fattoush   Serves 1

Here's a great way to use up pita bread before it gets stale.

2 cups chopped romaine lettuce
3 radishes, chopped
1 tablespoon chopped onion
1 tomato, chopped
½ cup chopped cucumber
¼ cup chopped parsley

¼ cup chopped green pepper
1 pita bread, toasted and rubbed
  with a cut garlic clove
2 teaspoons lemon juice
1 tablespoon extra-virgin olive oil
¼ cup crumbled feta cheese (or
  crumbled baked tofu)

Combine the lettuce, radishes, onion, tomato, cucumber, parsley, and green
pepper in a bowl and toss gently. Tear the pita bread into small bits, add to
the salad, and toss again. Sprinkle the salad with the lemon juice and olive
oil and serve.

Pasta with Spinach   Serves 4

Use other greens such as baby kale or sliced Swiss chard in place of the
spinach, if you wish.

8 ounces whole grain rotini or ziti
2 tablespoons extra-virgin olive oil
2 cloves garlic, minced
1 15-ounce can cannellini beans,
  drained and rinsed

4 cups chopped baby spinach leaves
½ cup shredded Asiago cheese
  (optional)
Salt and freshly ground black
  pepper to taste

Bring a large pot of water to a boil, add the pasta, and cook according to
the package directions. Drain and set aside. Heat the olive oil in a skillet and
sauté the garlic for 3 minutes. Add the beans, pasta, and spinach and heat
for a few minutes, just until the greens are wilted but still bright green.
Sprinkle with the cheese (if using), season with salt and pepper, toss, and
serve.

Day 25

Breakfast ① whole grains ② fruit/vegetables ③ protein

①②③ ½ cup granola, ¼ cup chopped walnuts, and 1 cup dairy or plant-based milk

② ½ cup peach slices

Early Grey tea (optional milk, dairy or plant-based)

Lunch

Caprese Salad

1 cup vegetable soup

1 whole grain roll with 2 tablespoons almond butter

OR Leftovers: Reheat **Pasta with Spinach** from Day 24 dinner.

½ cup grapes

Coffee (optional milk, dairy or plant-based)

Dinner

Brussels Sprouts with Wheat Berries

1 cup romaine lettuce with whole grain croutons, cherry tomatoes, and **Vinaigrette** (page 70)

½ cup papaya chunks

Chamomile tea

Tip

Build-Your-Own Salad
One of the healthiest – and most delicious – plant-based meals can be made in mere minutes. Put a handful of salad greens on your plate and top with your favorite add-ons, including canned beans, cooked whole grains, chopped vegetables, chopped fruit, dried fruit, nuts, seeds, and olives. Then drizzle with a simple vinaigrette (page 70) or a flavored vinegar.

Recipes

Caprese Salad   Serves 4

For the best flavor, rely on home-grown or farmers market ripe tomatoes.

4 cups arugula
2 tomatoes, sliced
8 ounces soft mozzarella or plant-based cheese, sliced
¼ cup fresh basil leaves
1 tablespoon extra-virgin olive oil
1 tablespoon balsamic vinegar
Salt and pepper to taste

Line a salad platter with the arugula. Arrange the tomato slices and mozzarella slices on top of the arugula. Sprinkle with the basil leaves and drizzle with the olive oil and vinegar. Season with salt and pepper and serve.

Brussels Sprouts with Wheat Berries   Serves 4

If you think you don't like Brussels sprouts, try them in this delicious dish.

1 pound fresh Brussels sprouts, cleaned and halved
1 8-ounce package seitan, cut into strips
1 cup mushrooms, sliced
⅓ cup chopped hazelnuts
Juice of ½ lemon
1 tablespoon extra-virgin olive oil
¼ teaspoon black pepper
½ teaspoon dried sage
Pinch of sea salt
2 cups cooked wheat berries (cooked according to package directions)

Preheat the oven to 375°F. Place the Brussels sprouts in a baking dish. Add the seitan, mushrooms, and hazelnuts and stir lightly. Drizzle with the lemon juice and olive oil. Season with black pepper, sage, and sea salt. Toss and roast until tender and browned, about 30 minutes. Serve hot, with wheat berries.

Day 26

Breakfast ① whole grains ② fruit/vegetables ③ protein

① 2 slices whole grain toast

②③ **Southwest Tofu Scramble**

② ½ cup orange juice

  Coffee (optional milk, dairy or plant-based)

Lunch

  1 veggie burger with whole grain bun, tomato slices, and lettuce

  1 cup tomato-vegetable soup

  OR Leftovers: Reheat **Brussels Sprouts with Wheat Berries** from
    Day 25 dinner.

  ½ cup apricots

  Iced tea

Dinner

  Lentil Stew

  1 slice whole grain flatbread

  1 cup cucumber-tomato-parsley salad

  ½ cup dried figs and pistachios

  Red tea

Tip

How to Press Tofu
Removing excess liquid from tofu makes it firmer and allows it
to absorb all the flavors in a dish. Simply place a block of tofu
on a plate lined with several layers of paper towels, cover with
another plate and something heavy (like a large can of tomatoes), and set aside for about 30 minutes to allow the extra liquid
to drain off.

Recipes

Southwest Tofu Scramble   Serves 4

Make this on a weekend morning when there's time to linger.

1-2 teaspoons cumin
2 teaspoons reduced-sodium
  soy sauce
2 tablespoons nutritional yeast
1 14-ounce package firm tofu,
  drained

2 teaspoons extra-virgin olive oil
1 zucchini, diced
½ cup sliced mushrooms
1 onion, sliced

Combine the cumin, soy sauce, and nutritional
yeast in a bowl and mix with a fork until well
blended. Crumble the tofu into the bowl and
toss gently to coat all the crumbles. Heat the
olive oil in a heavy skillet, add the zucchini, mushrooms, and onion, and
sauté over medium heat for about 5 minutes. Add the tofu, reduce the heat
to medium-low, and continue cooking for about 10 minutes, turning the
tofu with a spatula as needed, until it is slightly crusty and browned.
Serve hot.

Lentil Stew   Serves 4

Just learning about lentils? This easy recipe is a great place to discover their
delicious, earthy flavor.

1 onion, diced
2 cloves garlic, minced
1 red potato, peeled and diced
1 carrot, sliced
1 bell pepper, diced
1 cup uncooked lentils
1 14.5-ounce can diced tomatoes,
  with juice

3 cups water
¾ teaspoon paprika
¼ teaspoon cayenne pepper
1 teaspoon cumin
½ teaspoon cinnamon
¼ cup fresh chopped parsley

Combine all the ingredients except the parsley in a large pot. Stir well, bring
just to a boil, reduce the heat to medium-low, cover, and cook for about 45
minutes, until the lentils are tender. Add the parsley. Serve hot.

Day 27

Breakfast ① whole grains ② fruit/vegetables ③ protein

①②③ 2 small buckwheat pancakes from mix topped with ½ cup blueberries and 2 tablespoons chopped pecans

Darjeeling tea (optional milk, dairy or plant-based)

Lunch

Vegetable-noodle soup

Three-Bean Salad

OR Leftovers: Reheat **Lentil Stew** from Day 26 dinner.

1 slice whole grain crispbread with 1 tablespoon peanut butter

1 banana

Iced herbal tea

Dinner

Ratatouille

½ cup roasted potatoes

1 cup Caesar salad with 1 ounce Parmesan cheese or ½ cup baked tofu, 1 tablespoon capers, ¼ cup croutons, and **Vinaigrette** (page 70)

2 plums

Tip

Get Nutty!
Walnuts, almonds, pistachios, and peanuts, plus seeds, including sesame, sunflower, hemp, and pumpkin, are great sources of nutrients. They are rich in protein, vitamins, minerals, fiber, and healthy fats. Enjoy at least one serving (about ¼ cup) every day.

Recipes

Three-Bean Salad   Serves 6

Make this deli favorite yourself to assure clean, fresh flavors.

1 15-ounce can kidney beans, drained and rinsed
1 15-ounce can chickpeas, drained and rinsed
2 cups frozen green beans, thawed
1 small jar roasted red bell peppers, drained
4 scallions, diced

1 tablespoon extra-virgin olive oil
2 tablespoons red-wine vinegar
½ teaspoon garlic powder
½ teaspoon dried oregano
Salt and freshly ground black pepper to taste
Salad greens, as needed

Combine the kidney, garbanzo, and green beans in a bowl. Stir in the peppers and scallions. In a small bowl whisk together the oil, vinegar, garlic powder, oregano, and salt and pepper. Stir the dressing into the beans. Serve on salad greens.

Ratatouille   Serves 8

For a heartier dish, add a can of drained, rinsed beans for the last 10 minutes of cooking time.

1 tablespoon extra-virgin olive oil
1 onion, diced
2 cloves garlic, minced
1 eggplant, diced
2 zucchini, diced
1 bell pepper, diced
1 teaspoon dried oregano
Salt and freshly ground black pepper to taste

1 14.5-ounce can diced tomatoes, with juice
1 cup tomato sauce
1 cup shredded Pecorino or plant-based cheese

Preheat the oven to 350°F. Heat the olive oil in a large skillet and sauté the onion and garlic for 7 minutes. Add the eggplant, zucchini, and pepper, and sauté for 5 minutes. Stir in the seasonings, diced tomatoes, and tomato sauce, and cook for an additional 1 or 2 minutes. Transfer to a large casserole dish and bake for about 35 minutes, uncovered, until tender. Sprinkle with cheese and serve hot.

Day 28

Breakfast ① whole grains ② fruit/vegetables ③ protein

①③ 1 whole grain biscuit (from mix) with 2 tablespoons sunflower seed butter

② ½ cup strawberries, fresh or frozen

Peppermint tea

Lunch

Vegetable Sushi

1 cup miso soup

3–4 (1 ounce) sesame crackers

OR Leftovers: Reheat **Ratatouille** from Day 27 dinner.

6 ounces yogurt (dairy or soy) with ½ cup mandarin orange or clementine segments

Green tea

Dinner

Squash-Quinoa Boats

½ cup garbanzo beans

½ cup sautéed Swiss chard with garlic

1 whole grain dinner roll

½ cup grapes

Iced mango tea

Tip

Stuffed Veggies

Use vegetables such as bell peppers, acorn or delicata or summer squash to make main course "boats." Fill them with mixtures of cooked whole grains, diced cooked vegetables, currants, and chopped nuts and bake at 350°F for about 30 minutes. Top with a spoonful of pesto or hummus.

Recipes

Vegetable Sushi
Serves 8

Master this technique and experiment with your favorite vegetables.

1 cup uncooked short-grain brown rice

1 tablespoon reduced-sodium soy sauce

2 tablespoons rice vinegar

1 teaspoon honey or agave nectar

4 sheets nori (toasted seaweed)

Assorted vegetables, thinly sliced, including carrots, scallions, avocado, cucumber, asparagus, cabbage, mushrooms, and bell pepper

2 teaspoons sesame seeds

Cook the rice according to the package directions. Stir in the soy sauce, vinegar, and honey. Set aside until cool. Spread ¾ cup of rice on a nori sheet, top with your choice of sliced vegetables, and sprinkle with sesame seeds. Roll tightly and slice with a sharp knife. Repeat to make 4 rolls. Serve with soup or salad.

Squash-Quinoa Boats
Serves 4

Top with edamame hummus or guacamole.

¼ cup uncooked quinoa

1 teaspoon vegetable bouillon

2 delicata squash

1 teaspoon extra-virgin olive oil

1 onion, diced

1 red pepper, diced

½ cup finely chopped mushrooms

1 clove garlic, minced

Dash of black pepper

1 teaspoon dried cilantro

¼ cup finely chopped pecans

Rinse the quinoa, put it in a saucepan with the bouillon and 1 cup of water, bring to a boil, reduce the heat to medium-low, cover, and cook for 20 minutes. Set aside. Preheat the oven to 350°F. Slice the squash in half horizontally. Using a spoon, scoop out the interior, leaving about ¼ inch of flesh around the peel, to make the "boats." Arrange the squash halves in a baking dish, hollow side up. Heat the olive oil in a small skillet, add the onion, and sauté for 2 minutes. Add the pepper, mushrooms, and garlic and sauté for 4 minutes. Transfer the vegetable mixture to a medium bowl and add the cilantro, pecans, and cooked quinoa. Stir to combine. Spoon ¼ of the filling into each squash half. Add ½ cup water to the bottom of the baking dish, cover the dish with foil, and bake for 30 minutes. Remove the foil and bake for an additional 10 minutes. Serve hot.

Dressing Basics

You can make your own flavorful salad dressings with just the right amount of healthy fat and flavor, and without undesirable ingredients, such as sugar and chemicals. Drizzle a small amount (about 1 teaspoon per person) on your salad to give it pizzazz. Make vinegar-based dressings ahead and store in the refrigerator for up to two weeks.

Vinaigrette   Makes ¾ cup

¼ cup vinegar (cider or wine)   Salt and pepper to taste
½ cup extra-virgin olive oil

Combine all ingredients in a jar with a tight-fitting lid and shake until well blended.

Variations:

Honey-Mustard Vinaigrette
Add 1 minced clove garlic,
1 teaspoon Dijon mustard, and
1 teaspoon honey or agave nectar.

Balsamic Vinaigrette
Use balsamic vinegar.

Sesame Vinaigrette
Add 1 teaspoon soy sauce and
1 teaspoon toasted sesame seeds

Thai Vinaigrette
Substitute lime juice for the vinegar,
and add 1 tablespoon soy sauce,
½ teaspoon minced gingerroot,
½ teaspoon red chili flakes, and
1 teaspoon minced cilantro.

Herb Vinaigrette
Add 1 tablespoon fresh chopped herbs, such as basil, oregano, rosemary, parsley, or tarragon.

Hummus   Makes 2 cups, 8 servings (¼ cup each)

Every plant-based refrigerator should contain hummus. Use it as a nutrient-rich dip, spread, and topping for sandwiches, wraps, salads, and more. Try this easy recipe. Once you master it, experiment with other kinds of canned beans.

1 15-ounce can chickpeas, drained   2 tablespoons tahini or unsalted
  and rinsed   peanut butter
2 cloves garlic   1 teaspoon extra-virgin olive oil
2 tablespoons lemon juice   Salt and pepper to taste

Combine the beans, garlic, lemon juice, tahini, and oil in a blender. Process until smooth, adding a bit of water as needed for a spreading or dipping consistency. Season with salt and pepper.

Tips for Healthier Plant-Based Eating

Follow our favorite tips for eating a whole foods, plant-based diet packed with good nutrition and great flavor.

- **Make plants the center of your plate.** Gain inspiration for meal planning by focusing on whole plant foods, such as legumes, seasonal vegetables and fruits, and nuts.

- **Patronize your local farmers market.** You'll be inspired by the array of ripe, seasonal, local fruits and vegetables picked at their peak, which can be the basis for delicious vegetarian meals all week long.

- **Borrow from traditional flavors.** Some of the best vegetarian food on the planet comes from ethnic cuisines, including Mediterranean, Indian, Latin American, African, and Asian.

- **Make every bite count.** Don't waste your calories on vegetarian junk foods, such as cookies, snack bars, chips, and refined crackers. Instead, rely on whole, minimally processed foods, such as legumes, fruits, vegetables, and whole grains.

- **Stock up on canned beans.** Sure, you can soak beans and cook them up the next day, but a variety of canned beans – chickpeas, kidney beans, black beans, and cannellini beans – in your pantry will make plant-based eating easier.

- **Do dairy right.** If you're vegetarian, dairy foods can contribute important nutrients – protein, calcium, and vitamin D – to your day. Include low-fat milk, cottage cheese, and cheese in your diet every day. If you're vegan, try plant-based milks fortified with calcium and vitamin D, such as soy, almond, and coconut. Note that soy is the only plant-based milk that provides a good source of protein.

- **Keep it simple.** Vegetarian meals don't have to be overly complicated. They can be as easy as a bean burrito, a veggie burger, a hummus pita bread sandwich, or a green salad topped with a serving of whole grains.

- **Fresh isn't the only option.** Don't limit your plant-based eating to only fresh plant foods. Rely on frozen fruits and vegetables, canned fruits and vegetables, and dried fruits, beans, and grains, too.

A Guide to Whole Grains

What's a Whole Grain?

Whole grains have three edible parts: the outer bran layers, rich in fiber and B vitamins; the germ, full of antioxidants; and the starchy endosperm. If the bran and the germ (the healthiest parts) are removed, the grain is said to be refined. Refined grains are missing about two-thirds of many essential nutrients. Some grains are then enriched, but this returns only about five of the many missing nutrients.

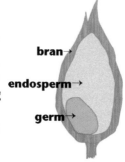

Your best bet for good health? Eat whole grains in all their glory – ground into flour, rolled into flakes, or mixed into pasta or bread. They are whole grains if all of the three original parts are still present in their original proportions.

Finding Whole Grains

Whole grains are an important component in plant-based diets. Barley, corn (including cornmeal and popcorn), oats (including oatmeal), quinoa, rice (both brown and colored), wheat (including farro and bulgur), and wild rice are among the whole grains sold in most supermarkets today. Look for breads, cereals, pastas, and other products that display the Whole Grain Stamp (above), which tells you how much whole grain is in a serving.

To learn more about whole grains, visit **wholegrainscouncil.org**.

Cooking Grains

Cooking grains is easy. Just bring some water or broth to a boil (usually about 2 cups for each cup of grain), add the grain, reduce the heat, cover, and simmer gently until all the water is absorbed. Cooking time varies from none – for fine bulgur or for couscous – to as much as an hour for grains like barley. Check the individual packages for more specific directions.

Barley: Look for hulled or hull-less barley; pearled barley is not a whole grain. Add barley to vegetable soups and stews, or combine with cucumbers, onions, and feta for a grain salad. Many people also make barley "risotto."

Bulgur: Bulgur can be finely ground or coarse. Coarse bulgur may need to be simmered for 5 minutes and then left covered for 20 minutes or so, to absorb its liquid. Fine bulgur can be simply added to boiling water or broth, then left covered for 20 minutes or more while you cook the rest of your meal. Mix with cooked vegetables to stuff peppers or squash, or simply enjoy it as a side dish.

Brown Rice: Use long grain for pilafs and short grain for creamy risottos. Look for red rice, black rice, and other colors that are also whole grain.

Couscous: Couscous is not a grain (there are no couscous plants) but rather a small pastalike granule made from either refined wheat or whole wheat. Look for the whole-wheat kind, and simply add boiling water, then let sit for 15 to 20 minutes. Serve with stews or curries.

Farro: Farro is a kind of wheat traditional to Italy. Look for whole farro (not pearled, or "semi-perlato"). Use it in salads, stews, or side dishes, or substitute it for oatmeal at breakfast.

Freekeh: This roasted green wheat has a smoky, nutty flavor and chewy texture. It's a nice change from brown rice. Serve with stews and curries.

Millet: A mild-flavored, gluten-free grain, millet can be used in pilafs, cereals, breads, soups, and stews.

Quinoa: Rinse several times in water to remove any bitter taste. If you're in a hurry, cook quinoa like pasta, in a generous amount of boiling water. Remove it as soon as it's tender.

Spelt: Look for the words "whole spelt" when buying this high-protein wheat. It has a mild, earthy flavor.

Tip

Planning Ahead
Prepare a large batch of whole grains ahead of time, store it in the refrigerator for up to three days (or freeze in 1 cup servings) and reheat what you need for a meal.

Plant Protein Guide

How do you fuel your vegetarian diet with protein? It's easy. Just make sure you include a serving of plant protein at each meal or snack.

Plant-Based Proteins	Serving Size	Calories	Protein	Fat	Sat Fat
Almonds	1 oz (approx. ¼ cup)	169	6 g	14 g	1 g
Black beans, cooked	½ cup	114	8 g	0.5 g	0 g
Black-eyed peas, cooked	½ cup	100	7 g	0.5 g	0 g
Brazil nuts*	1 oz (6–8 nuts)	190	4 g	19 g	5 g
Cashews	1 oz (approx. ¼ cup)	160	4 g	13 g	3 g
Chia seeds	1 oz (2½ tbsp)	137	4 g	9 g	1 g
Chickpeas (garbanzo beans), cooked	½ cup	135	8 g	2 g	0 g
Fava beans, cooked	½ cup	94	7 g	0.5 g	0 g
Flaxseeds	1 oz (3 tbsp)	150	5 g	12 g	1 g
Hazelnuts	1 oz (approx. ¼ cup)	181	4 g	17 g	1 g
Hemp seeds, shelled	1 oz (3 tbsp)	157	9 g	12 g	1 g
Kidney beans, cooked	½ cup	113	8 g	0.5 g	0 g
Lentils, cooked	½ cup	115	9 g	0.5 g	0 g
Macadamia nuts	1 oz (approx. ¼ cup)	203	2 g	21 g	3 g
Peanut butter	2 tbsp	188	8 g	16 g	3 g
Peanuts	1 oz (approx. ¼ cup)	164	7 g	14 g	2 g

Plant-Based Proteins	Serving Size	Calories	Protein	Fat	Sat Fat
Pecans	1 oz (approx. ¼ cup)	199	3 g	21 g	2 g
Pine nuts	1 oz (3 tbsp)	190	4 g	19 g	1 g
Pinto beans, cooked	½ cup	123	8 g	0.5 g	0 g
Pistachios	1 oz (approx. ¼ cup)	160	6 g	13 g	2 g
Pumpkin seeds (pepitas), hulled	1 oz (3 tbsp)	153	7 g	13 g	2 g
Seitan	½ cup	180	21 g	3 g	0 g
Sesame seeds	1 oz (3 tbsp)	160	5 g	14 g	2 g
Soybeans, cooked	½ cup	127	11 g	6 g	1 g
Split peas, cooked	½ cup	116	8 g	0.5 g	0 g
Sunflower seeds, hulled	1 oz (approx. ¼ cup)	163	5 g	14 g	2 g
Tempeh	½ cup	160	15 g	9 g	2 g
Tofu, regular, with added calcium	4 oz (½ cup)	94	10 g	6 g	1 g
Walnuts	1 oz (approx. ¼ cup)	190	4 g	18 g	2 g
White beans, cooked	½ cup	127	8 g	0.5 g	0 g

Source: Data from USDA National Nutrient Database for Standard Reference,
http://ndb.nal.usda.gov

Sat Fat = saturated fat; DV = daily value, based on 2,000 calories/day; oz = ounce; g = gram; tbsp = tablespoon

*Brazil nuts are very high in selenium. Avoid consuming large amounts on a regular basis.

Snacks at a Glance

Reach for one of these snacks, or a combination of several, if you want to expand your daily calorie intake. Add one of these foods to the daily menus as an afternoon pick-me-up, and/or as a dessert for lunch or dinner.

Note: The totals below reflect estimates. Check the specific nutrition labels on any products you purchase.

Snack	Serving Size	Calories	Fat (g)	Sat Fat (g)	Sodium (mg)	Carbs (g)	Fiber (g)	Protein (g)
Almonds	1 oz (approx. ¼ cup)	169	14	1	0	5	3	6
Apple	1 medium	80	0	0	0	21	4	0
Baba ghanoush	1 tbsp	20	1	0	25	2	1	1
Bean dip	2 tbsp	50	2.5	0	55	6	1	1
Biscotti	1 medium	100	5	1	50	11	2	6
Cantaloupe	1 cup	60	0	0	15	13	1	1
Cheese (Brie)	1 oz	95	8	5	120	0	0	6
Cheese (Feta)	1 oz	75	6	4	310	1	0	4
Cottage cheese	½ cup	80	1	1	460	3	0	14
Carrots (baby)	6	25	1	0	50	6	0	0
Cashews (raw)	1 oz (approx. ¼ cup)	160	13	3	90	9	1	5
Cherries	1 cup	90	0	0	5	19	3	1
Chocolate (dark)	1 oz	140	10	4	30	15	1	2
Cookies (oatmeal raisin)	2	210	7	2	200	20	2	3
Crackers (whole grain)	3	60	2	1	90	9	2	2
Dates	4	90	0	0	0	25	3	1
Figs (fresh)	2	70	0	0	0	19	3	1
Gelato (vanilla)	½ cup	140	9	5	40	10	0	3
Grapes	1 cup	100	0	0	0	25	1	1
Hummus (average)	1 tbsp	25	1	0	55	2	1	1

Snack	Serving Size	Calories	Fat (g)	Sat Fat (g)	Sodium (mg)	Carbs (g)	Fiber (g)	Protein (g)
Latte (with 1% milk)	1 cup	110	2	2	105	12	0	8
Mango	1 cup	110	0	0	0	28	3	1
Low-fat milk	1 cup	118	3	2	143	14	0	10
Olives (Kalamata)	6	40	3	0	220	3	1	0
Orange	1 medium	60	0	0	0	14	3	1
Peanuts (roasted, unsalted)	1 oz (approx. ¼ cup)	164	14	2	0	6	3	9
Peanut butter (smooth, unsalted)	2 tbsps	188	16	3	60	3	1	8
Pita bread	1 half	70	1	0	150	15	2	3
Pistachios	1 oz (approx. ¼ cup)	160	13	2	0	8	3	6
Popcorn (unbuttered)	2 cups	60	0	0	0	12	2	2
Sorbet (raspberry)	½ cup	100	0	0	0	15	1	0
Sunflower seeds (hulled, roasted, without salt)	1 oz (approx. ¼ cup)	163	14	2	0	7	3	6
Trail mix (average)	¼ cup	170	11	2	85	17	2	6
Yogurt, Greek (2%)	6 oz	130	3.5	2	70	7	0	17
Walnuts	1 oz (approx. ¼ cup)	190	18	2	0	4	2	4

Recipe Index and Nutritionals

Page	Recipe	Calories	Fat (g)	Sat Fat (g)	Sodium (mg)	Carbs (g)	Fiber (g)	Protein (g)
59	Asian Peanut Stir-Fry with Black Rice	381	14	2	381	42	10	18
49	Banana-Walnut Bread	162	7	1	63	23	3	4
59	Barley-Vegetable Soup	163	1	0	460	35	8	7
51	Barley with White Beans	178	3	1	184	33	9	9
41	Bean Burgers	191	8	1	182	23	3	4
19	Beet Salad	289	25	3	162	15	4	4
57	Black-Eyed Peas with Rice and Plantains	391	8	3	27	74	8	9
27	Bran-Raisin Muffins	161	6	5	119	27	3	4
29	Breakfast Smoothie	254	1	0	62	38	7	10
63	Brussels Sprouts	378	11	1	269	47	12	25
23	Camelback Chili	231	1	0	64	37	18	17
63	Caprese Salad	180	14	6.5	175	4	1	11
57	Cottage Cheese Pancakes	317	10	2	506	41	3	17
35	Curried Red Quinoa and Peach Salad	422	14	1	143	63	12	19
49	Dal with Rice	451	2	0	33	90	23	22
35	Enchilada Casserole	325	11	3.5	583	45	9	14
19	Farfalle with Avocado Sauce	378	12	2	19	60	11	10
55	Farmers Market Lasagna	200	7	3	460	25	5	10
37	Farro-Cabbage Salad	234	6	1	14	38	6	8
61	Fattoush	395	23	7	760	31	6	17

Recipe Index and Nutritionals

Page	Recipe	Calories	Fat (g)	Sat Fat (g)	Sodium (mg)	Carbs (g)	Fiber (g)	Protein (g)
21	French Potato Salad	96	7	1	90	7	1	1
70	Hummus	51	1	0	58	7	2	2
31	League of Nations Lentil Soup	185	3	0	305	31	12	10
65	Lentil Stew	252	1	0	240	48	4	15
21	Lentils with Sriracha Sauce	414	15	1.5	329	53	19	19
31	Manhattan Millet Cakes	252	10	3	487	33	5	9
53	Minnestrone	103	0	0	282	23	6	5
25	Oat Risotto with Fava Beans and Asparagus	375	6.5	.5	288	57	16	16
37	Pasta Pomodoro	291	9	1	252	45	8	10
47	Pasta Puttanesca	325	10	3	434	49	9	11
23	Pasta with Kale	410	15	1	52	55	9	13
61	Pasta with Spinach	348	9	1	264	60	12	14
51	Pasta with Roasted Vegetables	377	8	1	28	70	14	15
15	Pita Bread with Hummus and Garden Vegetables	394	14	2	452	60	10	12
39	Quick Coconut Curry with Rice	317	8	3	460	41	7	20
55	Quinoa-Spinach Salad	201	7	1	284	29	6	8
67	Ratatouille	95	4	2	465	12	4	6
43	Rice Taboulleh Salad	159	6	1	40	24	2	3
17	Scrambled Eggs with Cottage Cheese and Herbs	120	8	2	184	2	0	10
43	Shepherds Pie	492	16	3	303	75	16	15

Recipe Index and Nutritionals

Page	Recipe	Calories	Fat (g)	Sat Fat (g)	Sodium (mg)	Carbs (g)	Fiber (g)	Protein (g)
53	Sonoma Vegetable Skewers with Spelt	294	13	2	26	35	7	16
29	Southwestern Beans and Rice	297	2	0	426	53	16	17
65	Southwest Tofu Scramble	157	7	1	108	11	5	16
27	Spicy Thai Noodles	354	15	3	672	23	36	4
69	Squash-Quinoa Boats	180	8	1	190	29	4	5
45	Stir-Fry with Noodles	413	9	1	348	64	9	14
17	Sweet Potato Curry with Millet	400	14	2.5	398	60	10	13
33	Thai Peanut Wrap	497	23	5	425	49	14	27
67	Three-Bean Salad	191	4	0	434	29	9	9
39	Vegetable-Bean Stew	212	0	0	40	45	8	11
33	Vegetable Couscous	336	4	.5	425	64	14	10
15	Vegetable Stir-Fry 101	244	9	1	315	37	4	14
69	Vegetable Sushi	111	1	0	85	21	2	3
45	Veggie Pizza	217	7	3	331	28	3	12
25	Veggie Wrap	397	22	4	368	33	8	17
41	Vietnamese Noodle Soup	276	3	.5	425	52	4	10
70	Vinaigrette Dressings	81	9	1	13-50	0	0	0
47	Williamsburg Kale Salad	182	9	1	177	16	3	11

Index

Index

Index

Notes

Printed in Great Britain
by Amazon